HO CHI MINH
SELECTED ARTICLES AND SPEECHES

W9-BZF-559

HO CHI MINH
SELECTED ARTICLES
AND SPEECHES
1920–1967

Edited, with an Introduction, by
JACK WODDIS

INTERNATIONAL PUBLISHERS
New York

Publisher's Note

Since this book was first published, Ho Chi Minh died, September 3, 1969, at the age of 79. He was buried in Hanoi's Badinh Square, where independence was proclaimed in August 1945. His *Testament*, released after his death, has been added as an appendix to the present edition.

Printed in the United States of America

 159

CONTENTS

1920: Speech at the Tours Congress of the French Socialist Party 13
1922: Some Considerations on the Colonial Question .. 15
1923: The Counter-revolutionary Army 18
1924: Lynching 20
1930: Speech at the Founding of the Communist Party
of Indo-China 26
1941: Letter from Abroad 29
1945: Appeal for General Insurrection 32
Speech in the First Days of the Resistance War
in South Vietnam 34
1946: Message to the Vietnamese People, the French
People and the Peoples of the Allied Nations 36
1948: To the Congress of the National Committee of
the Viet Minh 39
1949: Message to Peasant Cadres 42
Letter to Catholic Compatriots 44
1951: Political Report at the 2nd National Congress of
the Vietnam Workers' Party (extract) 46
Message to Puppet Troops 55
Preface to "The Underground Party Committee" 57
1952: Imperialist Aggressors Can Never Enslave the
Heroic Vietnamese People (extracts) 59
Oppose Corruption 67
1953: Replies to a Swedish Correspondent 70
Land Reform (extract from Report to the Natio-
nal Assembly of the Democratic Republic of
Vietnam) 72
1954: Congratulatory Letter on the Victory at Dien
Bien Phu 79

The New Situation   80

Appeal Made after the Successful Conclusion of
the Geneva Agreements   91
The First Land Reform Drive at Thai Nguyen   94
1955: Speech at National Conference of Mutual Aid
Teams (extract)   97
Address to the Closing Session of the Vietnam
Fatherland Front Congress   99
1956: Mass Education   102
Talk with Intellectuals   107
1957: Speech Inaugurating the First Theoretical Course
of Nguyen Ai Quoc School   110

The October Revolution and The Liberation of
the Peoples of the East (extract)   113

1958: Talks at a Press Conference at Rangoon (extract) 121
Our Party   123
1959: The Draft Law on Marriage and the Family   129
Report on the Draft Amended Constitution
(extract)   131
1960: Thirty Years of Activity of the Vietnam Wor-
kers' Party   143
The Path which Led Me to Leninism   156
1965: Answers to the British "Daily Worker"   159
Reply to Professor Linus Pauling   162
1966: Letter to the Heads of State of the Soviet Union,
the People's Republic of China and the Other
Socialist Countries   166
1967: Reply to President Lyndon B. Johnson   170
Appendix: *The Last Testament of Ho Chi Minh*   173

INTRODUCTION

Ho Chi Minh, President of the Democratic Republic of Vietnam, celebrated his 79th birthday on May 19, 1969. For over fifty years he has been active in the revolutionary movement — in France, in Vietnam, in China, in the Soviet Union. Today, pictures of Uncle Ho, as he is commonly called in Vietnam, are carried in demonstrations from Tokyo to San Francisco, from Havana to Bombay. His name is acclaimed by marchers in London, Paris, Rome and Bonn.

Yet most people know very little about this remarkable man; and his ideas and views, as expressed in his writings and speeches, have been strangely neglected in the West.

Nguyen Tat Tanh (later to become known as Ho Chi Minh) was born in 1890, into the family of a poor peasant scholar in Kimlien hamlet, Namlien village, in the Namdan district of Nghean province. For generations the peasants of this province had struggled against poverty, against dispossession of their land, heavy taxation and forced labour.

The young Ho was greatly influenced by his surroundings and was stirred by the anti-colonial sentiments of his family and fellow villagers. He went to Hue in 1905 for his schooling but eventually became discontented with the character of the teaching, aimed so obviously at turning out loyal subjects of the colonial system. He then sought training in Saigon. Anxious to learn more about the world, he decided to visit France and other European countries, and obtained a job as a galleyhand on a French ship. He travelled widely in this way, visiting France, Great Britain, Germany, the United States and several French colonies in Africa.

This experience was never forgotten. The young Ho was able to learn, from first-hand experience, that workers everywhere suffered from exploitation by a handful of rich

7

people, who sat on the backs of their own workers as well as on those of the people in the colonies. From an early age, therefore, Ho Chi Minh learnt the lesson of internationalism, and became convinced as to the necessity of all working people uniting against their common enemy, imperialism. This idea, which runs like a thread through all his writings and speeches, was deepened still further by his experiences in the ensuing years.

When the first world war broke out, Ho Chi Minh was in Britain. He immediately went to France to contact Vietnamese patriots who were engaged in organising the struggle of their people against French domination. The October Revolution in Russia in 1917 had a decisive influence on Ho Chi Minh. He contacted Marxists in Paris, and joined the French Socialist Party, in which many French Marxists then worked. At the same time, he organised the Group of Vietnamese Patriots Living in France, on whose behalf he presented to the Versailles Peace Conference in 1919 an eight-point series of demands. It was during this period that Ho went under the name Nguyen Ai Quoc ('Nguyen the Patriot').

In 1920 he attended the Tours Congress of the French Socialist Party, at which a debate was held on the question of joining the newly established Communist International. Ho Chi Minh spoke in favour of joining, and the majority voted for such a decision. A French Communist Party was formed, and Ho Chi Minh became a foundation member.

With the help of the French Communist Party, he founded the League of Colonial Peoples, and published the journal, *Le Paria*, in which he poured out a series of articles sharply exposing the crimes of colonialism. In this period he wrote often on colonial questions for *Humanité*, for the trade union journal, *La Vie Ouvriere*, and for the international communist press. To this period, too, belongs his pamphlet, *French Colonisation on Trial*.

In 1924, Ho Chi Minh went to the Soviet Union to attend the Fifth Congress of the Communist International, held in Moscow. It is typical of his approach that before leaving

8

Paris for Moscow he wrote a letter to his friends from African colonies then living in France, urging them to "go back to their countries, make contact with the masses to awaken, organise, unite and train them, and lead them to fight for freedom and independence."

In the same year, he went to China, where he got in touch with a revolutionary Vietnamese organisation known as *Tam tam xa*. Together with members of this organisation he set up a Vietnam Revolutionary Youth League, and a League of Oppressed Asian Peoples. He stayed in Canton for the next few years, helping to train young Vietnamese students who had been expelled from school for participating in patriotic strikes in Vietnam. These students returned to Vietnam after training, to set up organisations of the Revolutionary Youth League. It was in this period that Ho Chi Minh wrote *The Road of the Revolution*, as a revolutionary manual. *Youth*, the journal of the Youth League, was also issued by him at this time.

The period 1927 to 1930 saw a big development of the revolutionary movement in Vietnam. The Revolutionary Youth League grew, strikes broke out in a number of places, and in 1929 the movement spread to the countryside, with peasants staging demonstrations against taxation and forced labour. The ideas of Marxism began to spread in the revolutionary organisations, and the first Communist cell was set up in North Vietnam.

In June 1929, the Indochinese Communist Party was founded in North Vietnam, from amongst members of the Youth League. Then followed the formation of the Annamese Communist Party in the South, and the Tan Viet Communist League in central and partly South Vietnam. Thus, there were three Communist Parties in Vietnam, each claiming to be the only genuinely revolutionary one, and criticising the other two. All three tried to contact the Communist International for recognition.

Ho Chi Minh was sent by the Communist International to discuss with the three parties the question of unification. He convened a unity conference in Hong Kong in 1930, at which the three Communist organisations were amalgamated into a single Vietnam Communist Party, later renamed the Indochinese Communist Party.

Ho Chi Minh continued working in China in 1930 and 1931, but he kept in close touch with events in Vietnam, giving constant advice by letter to the Central Committee of the Party. In June, 1931, he was arrested by the British authorities in Hongkong, but won his freedom (after an appeal to the Privy Council in London, in the preparation of which D. N. Pritt, K. C. played a part) and went to Shanghai.

In 1933 he studied at the Lenin School in the Soviet Union, where leading personnel of many Communist Parties received their training. In 1936 he returned to China. He still continued to maintain close and regular contact with political developments in Vietnam, and to send frequent letters to the Party and articles for its journals, and for those of the Democratic Front which had been set up following the electoral victory of the Popular Front in France.

At last, after his long absence, Ho Chi Minh returned to Vietnam in February 1941. In May, a special meeting of the Party's central committee was held in Pacbo, a remote jungle village in Caobang province, under the chairmanship of Ho Chi Minh. The call was made for the setting up of the League for the Independence of Vietnam, i.e. the Vietminh Front, paving the way for the armed insurrection against Japanese and French occupation, the winning of political power and the founding of the Democratic Republic of Vietnam. The policy decided on at this meeting under Ho's chairmanship led in August 1945 to the victory of the national revolution.

Previous to that, Ho Chi Minh stayed in Vietnam for a year, writing works on guerrilla warfare, and editing the journal, *Vietnam Doc Lap* (Independent Vietnam). In August 1942 he went to China to try to win support from the Chiang Kai-shek government, but was arrested and kept in jail for a year. It was in this period that he took the name of Ho Chi Minh. After his release he returned to Vietnam, visiting

China once again in 1944 before returning once more to his native land.

In May 1945 a National Conference of the Party and a People's Congress were held in Tantrao, a village in Tuyenquang province. The expansion of guerrilla warfare was decided on, and preparations made for a national uprising, and for the founding of a provisional Government. Ho Chi Minh was appointed president of the Provisional Government.

The Vietnam people rose in August 1945, and on August 19 took over the capital, Hanoi. On September 2, 1945, the Provisional Government presented itself before the people, and President Ho Chi Minh read the Proclamation of Independence at Badinh Square, in Hanoi. General elections took place on January 6, 1946, throughout the country, for a new National Assembly. A constitutional draft committee was set up, under Ho Chi Minh's chairmanship, and on March 2, 1946, the National Assembly adopted the first Constitution for independent Vietnam.

The next twenty-two years placed new strains on the Vietnamese people and their President. In the midst of overcoming the legacies of French colonialism and constructing socialism, they first had to fight against the attempt by France to re-occupy the territory; and then, after the defeat of the French in 1954, faced the consequences of the division of the country and repression in the south by successive puppet governments, propped up by U.S. bayonets and dollars. In the past few years, this has grown into a general war of the Vietnamese people against U.S. aggression. In all these difficult phases of reconstruction and struggle President Ho Chi Minh has remained as the leader and soul of the people's effort and resistance.

*

The principal writings and speeches of Ho Chi Minh available in English appear in a Four Volume edition of his Selected Works issued in Hanoi in the period 1960—1962. These selections cover a period from 1920 to 1960, and comprise no less than 1,269 pages. In addition, a volume of Ho Chi Minh's speeches and statements against U.S. aggression was issued in Hanoi in 1967, covering the period up till that year. With this volume of 152 pages, there are thus a total of 1,421 pages of the main works of Ho Chi Minh available in English.

The selection in this present book constitutes, therefore, only some ten per cent of what has been published. The selections have been chosen so as to cover the main periods of Ho Chi Minh's life and political activity, and to enable the reader to obtain an idea of his thoughts and outlook over a period of nearly fifty years.

Starting with his speech at the Tours Congress of the Socialist Party in 1920, the selection given here contains examples of his early writings in colonial questions.

The bulk of the selections reproduced here cover writings and speeches at each stage of the Vietnam struggle, including materials on the Communist Party, the struggle against Japan and France, Ho's attitude to the French people, to puppet troops, and Catholics, questions of land reform, cadres, bureaucracy, intellectuals, guerrilla warfare, mass education, marriage and the family, democracy, the Soviet Union, the October Revolution, Leninism, and key aspects of the liberation war against U.S. imperialism.

This short book is naturally only an introduction to the works of Ho Chi Minh; but it is hoped that, by giving within a limited compass extracts from his main articles and speeches, sufficient will be provided to give the reader an inkling of his main ideas and policies. We hope, too, that this book will act as a stimulus and encouragement to study further the work of this outstanding revolutionary.

JACK WODDIS

Speech at the Tours Congress

(delivered at the 18th Congress of the French Socialist Party, at Tours, December 1920)

Today, instead of contributing, together with you, to world revolution, I come here with deep sadness to speak as a member of the Socialist Party, against the imperialists who have committed abhorrent crimes on my native land.

You all have known that French imperialism entered Indo-China half a century ago. In its selfish interests, it conquered our country with bayonets. Since then we have not only been oppressed and exploited shamelessly, but also tortured and poisoned pitilessly. Plainly speaking, we have been poisoned with opium, alcohol, etc. I cannot, in some minutes, reveal all the atrocities that the predatory capitalists have inflcted on Indo-China. Prisons outnumber schools and are always overcrowded with detainees. Any natives having socialist ideas are arrested and sometimes murdered without trial. Such is the so-called justice in Indo-China. In that country the Vietnamese are discriminated against, they do not enjoy safety like Europeans or those having European citizenship. We have neither freedom of press nor freedom of speech. Even freedom of assembly and freedom of association donot exist. We have no right to live in other countries or to go abroad as tourists. We are forced to live in utter ignorance and obscurity because we have no right to study. In Indo-China the colonialists find all ways and means to force us to smoke opium and drink alcohol to poison and beset us. Thousands of Vietnamese have been led to a slow death or massacred to protect other people's interests.

Comrades, such is the treatment inflicted upon more than twenty million Vietnamese, that is more than half the population of France. And they are said to be under French protection. The socialist Party must act practically to support the oppressed natives.

The Party must make propaganda for socialism in all colonial countries. We have realized that the Socialist Party's joining the Third International means that it has practically promised that from now on it will correctly assess the importance of the colonial question. We are very glad to learn that a Standing Delegation has been appointed to study the North Africa question and in the near future we will be very glad if the Party sends one of its members to Indo-China to study on-the-spot the questions relating to this country, and the activities which should be carried out there.

On behalf of the whole of mankind, on behalf of all the Socialist Party's members, both left and right wings, we call upon you ! Comrades, save us !

SOME CONSIDERATIONS ON THE COLONIAL QUESTION

(article in L' H u m a n i t e, Paris, May 25, 1922)

Since the French Party has accepted Moscow's twenty-one conditions and joined the Third International, among the problems which it has set itself is a particularly ticklish one — colonial policy. Unlike the First and Second Internationals it cannot be satisfied with purely sentimental expressions of position leading to nothing at all, but must have a well defined working programme, an effective and practical policy.

On this point, more than on others, the Party faces many difficulties, the greatest of which are the following:

1. *The great size of the colonies.*

Not counting the new 'trusteeships' acquired after the war, France possesses:

In Asia, 450,000 square kilometres, in Africa 3,541,000 square kilometres, in America, 108,000 square kilometres and in Oceania, 21,600 square kilometres, or a total area of 4,120,000 square kilometres (eight times its own territory), with a population of 48,000,000 souls. These people speak over twenty different languages. This diversity of tongues does not make propaganda easy, for, except in a few old colonies, a French propagandist can make himself understood only through an interpreter. However, translations are of limited value, and in these countries of administrative despotism, it is rather difficult to find an interpreter to translate revolutionary speeches.

There are other drawbacks: though the natives of all the colonies are equally oppressed and exploited, their intellectual, economic and political development differs greatly from one region to another. Between Annam and the Congo, Martinique and New Caledonia, there is absolutely nothing in common, except poverty.

2. *The indifference of the proletariat of the mother country towards the colonies.*

In his theses on the colonial question, Lenin clearly stated that the workers of colonizing countries are bound to give the most active assistance to the liberation movements in subject countries. To this end, the workers of the mother country must know what a colony really is, they must be acquainted with what is going on there, and with the suffering — a thousand times more acute than theirs — endured by their brothers, the proletarians in the colonies. In a word, they must take an interest in this question.

Unfortunately, there are many militants who still think that a colony is nothing but a country with plenty of sand underfoot and of sun overhead; a few green coconut palms and coloured folk, that is all. And they take not the slightest interest in the matter.

3. *The ignorance of the natives.*

In colonized countries — in old Indo-China as well as in new Dahomey — the class struggle, and proletarian strength, are unknown factors for the simple reason that there are neither big commercial and industrial enterprises, nor workers' organisations. In the eyes of the natives, Bolshevism — a word which is the more vivid and expressive because frequently used by the bourgeoisie — means either the destruction of everything or emancipation from the foreign yoke. The first sense given to the word drives the ignorant and timorous masses away from us; the second leads them to nationalism. Both senses are equally dangerous. Only a tiny section of the intelligentsia knows what is meant by communism. But these gentry, belonging to the native bourgeoisie and supporting the bourgeois colonialists, have no interest in the communist doctrine being understood and propagated. On the contrary, like the dog in the fable, they prefer to bear the mark of the collar and to have their piece of bone. Generally speaking, the masses are thoroughly rebellious, but completely ignorant. They want to free themselves, but do not know how to go about doing so.

4. *Prejudices*

The mutual ignorance of the two proletariats gives rise to prejudices. The French workers look upon the native as an inferior and negligible human being, incapable of understanding and still less of taking action. The natives regard all the French as wicked exploiters. Imperialism and capitalism do not fail to take advantage of this mutual suspicion and this artificial racial hierarchy to frustrate propaganda nad divide forces which ought to unite.

5. *Fierceness of repression*

If the French colonialists are unskilful in developing colonial resources, they are masters in the art of savage repression and the manufacture of loyalty made to measure. The Gandhis and the de Valeras would have long since entered heaven had they been born in one of the French colonies. Surrounded by all the refinements of courts martial and special courts, a native militant cannot educate his oppressed and ignorant brothers without the risk of falling into the clutches of his civilisers.

Faced with these difficulties, what must the Party do? Intensify propaganda to overcome them.

The Counter-revolutionary Army

(article in La Vie Ouvrière, Paris, September 7, 1923)

We are aware that colonial rivalry was one of the main causes of the 1914—1918 imperialist war.

What all Frenchmen should realise, is that colonial expeditions are largely responsible for aggravating the depopulation from which their country is now suffering. If one looks at the statistics of military losses in killed and wounded sustained in the colonies, one is frightened by the gap they have caused in an ever decreasing population such as that of France. From January to June, 1923, in Morocco alone, 840 soldiers were killed or wounded for the greater glory of Marshal Lyautey !

What the French working class must realise, is that colonialism relies on the colonies to defeat all attempts at emancipation on the part of the working class. No longer having absolute confidence in the white soldiers, who are more or less contaminated by the idea of classes, French militarism uses African and Asian natives in their stead. Out of 159 regiments in the French Army, 10 are composed of colonial whites, i.e., semi-natives, 30 of Africans and 39 of natives from other colonies. One half of the French army is thus recruited in the colonies.

Now, an Annamese soldier is in service for four years and an Algerian for three years. Thus, according to the reckoning of French militarism, two native soldiers are worth almost five French.

Moreover, being ignorant of the language and politics of the country, thinking that all whites belong to the race of his exploiters, and finally spurred on by his white superiors,

18

the native soldier will march forward submissively and blindly, where the French soldier, more conscious, might refuse to go. Therein lies the danger.

One wonders for what reason 31 of the native regiments will be stationed on French territory? For what purpose are they intended? Are the French going to be civilised by these natives? The intention of French capitalism is thus clear. It is up to the French workers to act. They should fraternise with the native soldiers. They should make them understand that the workers of the mother country and the soldiers from the colonies are equally oppressed and exploited by the same masters, that they are all brothers of the same class, and that when the hour of struggle strikes, they will have, one and the other, to struggle against their common masters, and not between brothers.

LYNCHING

A little known aspect of American civilisation

*(article in L a   C o r r e s p o n d e n c e   I n t e r n a t i o n -
a l e , No. 59, 1924)*

It is well known that the black race is the most oppressed
and most exploited of the human family. It is well known
that the spread of capitalism and the discovery of the New
World had as an immediate result the rebirth of slavery
which was, for centuries, a scourge for the Negroes and a
bitter disgrace for mankind. What everyone does not per-
haps know, is that after 65 years of so-called emancipation,
American Negroes still endure atrocious moral and material
sufferings, of which the most cruel and horrible is the custom
of *lynching*.

The word lynching comes from Lynch. Lynch was the name
of a planter in Virginia, a landlord and judge. Availing
himself of the troubles of the War of Independence he took
the control of the whole district into his hands. He inflicted
the most savage punishment, without trial or process of
law. Thanks to the slave-traders, the Ku-Klux-Klan and
other secret societies, the illegal and barbarous practice of
lynching is spreading and continuing widely in the States
of the American Union. It has become more inhuman since
the emancipation of the Blacks, and is especially directed at
the latter.

Imagine a furious horde. Fists clenched, eyes bloodshot,
mouths foaming, yells, insults, curses ... This horde is
transported with the wild delight of a crime to be committed
without risk. They are armed with sticks, torches, revolvers,
ropes, knives, scissors, vitriol, daggers, in a word with all
that can be used to kill or wound.

20

Imagine in this human sea a flotsam of black flesh pushed about, beaten, trampled underfoot, torn, slashed, insulted, tossed hither and thither, bloodstained, dead.

The horde are the lynchers. The human rag is the Black, the victim.

In a wave of hatred and bestiality, the lynchers drag the Black to a wood or a public place. They tie him to a tree, pour kerosene over him, cover him with inflammable material. While waiting for the fire to be kindled, they smash his teeth, one by one. Then they gouge out his eyes. Little tufts of crinkly hair are torn from his head, carrying away with them bits of skin, baring a bloody skull. Little pieces of flesh come off his body, already contused from the blows.

The Black can no longer shout: his tongue has been swollen by a red hot iron. His whole body ripples, trembling, like a half crushed snake. A slash with a knife: one of his ears falls to the ground . . . Oh! How black he is! How awful! And the ladies tear at his face . . .

'Light up', shouts someone — 'Just enough to cook him slowly', adds another.

The Black is roasted, browned, burnt. But he deserves to die twice instead of once. He is therefore hanged, or more exactly, what is left of his corpse is hanged. And all those who were not able to help with the cooking applaud now.

Hurrah!

When everybody has had enough, the corpse is brought down. The rope is cut into small pieces which will be sold for three or five dollars each. Souvenirs and lucky charms quarrelled over by ladies.

'Popular justice', as they say over there, has been done. Calmed down, the crowd congratulate the 'organisers', then stream away slowly and cheerfully, as if after a feast, making appointments with one another for the next time.

While on the ground, stinking of fat and smoke, a black head, mutilated, roasted, deformed, grins horribly and seems to ask the setting sun, "Is this civilisation?"

21

From 1889 to 1919, 2,600 Blacks were lynched, including 51 women and girls and ten former Great War soldiers.

Among 78 Blacks lynched in 1919, 11 were burnt alive, three burnt after having been killed, 31 shot, three tortured to death, one cut into pieces, one drowned, and 11 put to death by various means.

Georgia heads the list with 22 victims, Mississipi follows with 12. Both have also three lynched soldiers to their credit. Of 11 burnt alive, the first State has four and the second two. Out of 34 cases of systematic, premeditated and organised lynching, it is still Georgia that holds first place with five. Mississipi comes second with three.

Among the charges brought against the victims of 1919, we note:

One of having been a member of the League of Non-Partisans (independent farmers);

One of having distributed revolutionary publications;

One of expressing his opinion on lynchings too freely;

One of having criticised the clashes between Whites and Blacks in Chicago;

One of having been known as a leader of the cause of the Blacks;

One for not getting out of the way and thus frightening a white child who was in a motor car.

In 1920, there were 50 lynchings, and in 1923, 28.

These crimes were all motivated by economic jealousy. Either the Negroes in the place were more prosperous than the Whites, or the black workers would not let themselves be exploited thoroughly. In all cases, the principal culprits were never troubled, for the simple reason that they were always incited, encouraged, spurred on, then protected, by the politicians, financiers and authorities, and above all by the reactionary press.

When a lynching was to take place or had taken place, the press seized upon it as a good occasion to increase sales.

22

The affair would be reported with a wealth of detail. Not the slightest reproach to the criminals. Not a word of pity for the victims. Not a commentary.

The *New Orleans States* of June 26, 1919, published a headline running right across the front page in letters five inches high: "Today a Negro Will be Burnt by 3,000 Citizens". And immediately underneath, in very small print: "Under a strong escort, the Kaiser has taken flight with the Crown Prince."

The *Jackson Daily News* of the same date, published across the first two columns of its front page in big letters:

Negro J. H. to be Burnt

by the Crowd at Ellistown

this afternoon at 5 p.m.

The newspaper only neglected to add, "The whole population is earnestly invited to attend." But the spirit was there.

A few details

"This evening at 7.40 p.m. J. H. was tortured with a red hot iron bar, then burnt ... A crowd of more than 2,000 people ... many women and children, were present at the incineration ... After the Negro had been bound from behind, a fire was kindled. A little further away, another fire was kindled in which an iron bar was placed. When it was red hot, a man took it and applied it to the Black's body. The latter, terrified, seized the iron with his hands, and the air was immediately filled with the smell of burning flesh ... The red hot iron having been applied to several parts of his body, his shouts and groans were heard as far away as in the town. After several minutes of torture, masked men poured petrol on him and set fire to the stake. The flames rose and enveloped the Negro who implored to be finished off with a shot. His supplications provoked shouts of derision"

(Chatanooga Times, February 13, 1918)

23

"15,000 people, men, women and children, applauded when petrol was poured over the Negro and the fire lit. They struggled, shouted and pushed one another to get nearer the Black . . . Two of them cut off his ears while the fire began to roast him.

"Another tried to cut off his heels . . . The crowd surged and changed places so that every one could see the Negro burn. When the flesh was entirely burnt, the bones laid bare and what had been a human being was but a smoking and deformed rag curling up in the flames, everyone was still there to look . . ."

(Memphis Press, May 22, 1917)

". . . men of all social classes, women and children, were present at the scene. Many ladies of high society followed the crowd from outside the prison, others joined it from neighbouring terraces . . . When the Negro's corpse fell, the pieces of rope were hotly contended for".

(Vicheburg Evening Post, May 4, 1919.)

". . . someone cut off his ears, another removed his sexual organ . . . He tried to cling to the rope, his fingers were cut off. While he was being hoisted to a tree, a giant of a man stabbed his neck; he received at least 25 wounds.

". . . he was several times hoisted up, then pulled down into the brazier. Finally a man caught him in a lasso, the end of which was attached to a horse which dragged the corpse through the streets of Waco. The tree on which the hanging took place, was right under a window of the mayor's house. The latter looked on while the crowd was in action. All along the way, everyone took part in the mutilation of the Negro. Some struck him with shovels, pickaxes, bricks, sticks. The body was covered with wounds from head to foot. A shout of joy escaped from thousands of throats when the fire was kindled. Some time after, the corpse was hoisted up in the air, so that everyone could look at it, which raised a storm of applause . . ."

(Crisis, July 1916.)

It is not only the Blacks, but also the Whites who dare to defend them, such as Mrs. Harriet Beecher Stowe — author of *Uncle Tom's Cabin* — who are ill-treated. Elijah Lovejoy was killed, John Brown hanged. Thomas Beach and Stephen Foster were persecuted, attacked and imprisoned. Here is what Foster wrote from prison, "When I look at my damaged limbs, I think that, to hold me, prison will not be necessary for much longer ... These last 15 months, their cells have been opened to me four times, 24 times my compatriots have dragged me out of their churches, twice they have thrown me from the second floor of their houses, they have damaged my kidneys once; another time they tried to put me in irons; twice they have made me pay fines; once 10,000 people tried to lynch me, and dealt me 20 blows on my head, arms and neck ..."

In 30 years, 708 Whites, including 11 women, have been lynched. Some for having organised strikes, others for having espoused the cause of the Blacks.

Among the collection of the crimes of American "civilisation' lynching has a place of honour.

SPEECH AT THE FOUNDING OF THE COMMUNIST PARTY OF INDO-CHINA

(delivered at Hong Kong, February 18, 1930)

Workers, peasants, soldiers, youth and pupils!

Oppressed and exploited compatriots!

Imperialist contradictions were the cause of the 1914—1918 World War. After this horrible slaughter, the world was divided into two camps: one is the revolutionary camp including the oppressed colonies and the exploited working class throughout the world. The vanguard force of this camp is the Soviet Union. The other is the counter-revolutionary camp of international capitalism and imperialism whose general staff is the League of Nations.

During this World War, various nations suffered untold losses in property and human lives. The French imperialists were the hardest hit. Therefore, in order to restore the capitalist forces in France, the French imperialists have resorted to every underhand scheme to intensify their capitalist exploitation in Indo-China. They set up new factories to exploit the workers with low wages. They plundered the peasants' land to establish plantations and drove them to utter poverty. They levied many heavy taxes. They imposed public loans upon our people. In short, they reduced us to wretchedness. They increased their military forces, firstly to strangle the Vietnamese revolution, secondly to prepare for a new imperialist war in the Pacific aimed at capturing new colonies, thirdly to suppress the Chinese revolution, fourthly to attack the Soviet Union because the latter helps the revolution of the oppressed nations and the exploited working class.

World War Two will break out. When it breaks, the French imperialists will certainly drive our people to a more horrible slaughter. If we give them a free hand to prepare for this war, suppress the Chinese revolution and attack the Soviet Union, if we give them a free hand to stifle the Vietnamese revolution, it is tantamount to giving them a free hand to wipe our race off the face of the earth and drown our nation in the Pacific.

However, the French imperialists' barbarous oppression and ruthless exploitation have awakened our compatriots who have all realised that revolution is the only road to life, without it they will die out piecemeal. This is the reason why the Vietnamese revolutionary movement has grown ever stronger with each passing day. The workers refuse to work, the peasants demand land, the pupils strike, the traders boycott. Everywhere the masses have risen to oppose the French imperialists.

The Vietnamese revolution has made the French imperialists tremble with fear. On the one hand, they utilise the feudalists and comprador bourgeois in our country to oppress and exploit our people. On the other, they terrorise, arrest, jail, deport and kill a great number of Vietnamese revolutionaries. If the French imperialists think that they can suppress the Vietnamese revolution by means of terrorist acts, they are utterly mistaken. Firstly, it is because the Vietnamese revolution is not isolated but enjoys the assistance of the world proletarian class in general and of the French working class in particular. Secondly, while the French imperialists are frenziedly carrying out terrorist acts, the Vietnamese Communists, formerly working separately, have now united into a single party, the Communist Party of Indo-China, to lead our entire people in their revolution.

Workers, peasants, soldiers, youth, pupils!

Oppressed and exploited compatriots!

The Communist Party of Indo-China is founded. It is the Party of the working class. It will help the proletarian class to lead the revolution in order to struggle for all the oppressed and exploited people. From now on we must join the Party, help it and follow it in order to implement the following slogans:

* To overthrow French imperialism, feudalism and the reactionary Vietnamese capitalist class.

* To make Indo-China completely independent.

* To establish a worker-peasant and soldier government.

* To confiscate the banks and other enterprises belonging to the imperialists and put them under the control of the worker-peasant and soldier government.

* To confiscate the whole of the plantations and property belonging to the imperialists and the Vietnamese reactionary capitalist class and distribute them to poor peasants.

* To implement the 8 hours working day.

* To abolish public loans and poll-tax. To waive unjust taxes hitting the poor people.

* To bring back all freedoms to the masses.

* To carry out universal education.

* To implement equality between man and woman.

LETTER FROM ABROAD

(June 6, 1941)

Elders!

Prominent personalities!

Intellectuals, peasants, workers, traders and soldiers!

Dear compatriots!

Since the French were defeated by the Germans, their forces have been completely disintegrated. However, with regard to our people, they continue to plunder us pitilessly, suck all our blood, and carry out a barbarous policy of all-out terrorism and massacre. Concerning their foreign policy, they bow their heads and kneel down, shamelessly cutting our land for Siam; without a single word of protest, they heartlessly offer our interests to Japan. As a result our people suffer under a double yoke: they serve not only as buffaloes and horses to the French invaders but also as slaves to the Japanese plunderers. Alas! What sin have our people committed to be doomed to such a wretched plight!

Living in such painful and lamentable conditions, can our people bind their own hands and doom themselves to death! No! Certainly not! More than twenty million sons and daughters of Lac Hong are resolute to do away with slavery. For nearly eighty years under the French invaders' iron heel we have unceasingly sacrificed ourselves and struggled for national independence and freedom. The loyal and heroic spirit of our predecessors such as Phan Dinh Phung, Hoang Hoa Tham and Luong Ngoc Quyen is still alive, the heroic feats of our revolutionaries in Thai Nguyen, Yen Bai, Nghe An and Ha Tinh provinces remain for ever in our memory. The recent uprising in the South and at Do Luong and Bac Son have testified to the determination of our compatriots to shed their blood as their glorious predecessors did, heroically to annihilate the enemy. If we did not succeed, it was not because the French invaders were strong, but only because the situation was not yet ripe and our compatriots throughout the country did not yet have the same heart and mind.

Now, the opportunity has come for our liberation. France itself is unable to dominate our country. As to the Japanese, on the one hand they are bogged down in China, on the other, they are hamstrung by the British and American forces, and certainly cannot use all their forces to contend with us. If our entire people are united and single-minded, we are certainly able to smash the picked French and Japanese armies.

Compatriots throughout the country ! Rise up quickly ! Let us follow the heroic example of the Chinese people ! Rise up quickly to organise the Association for National Salvation to fight the French and the Japanese.

Elders !

Prominent personalities !

Some hundreds of years ago, when our country was endangered by the Mongolian invasion, our elders under the Tran dynasty rose up in indignation and called on their sons and daughters throughout the country to rise as one in order to kill the enemy. Finally they saved their people from danger and their good name will be carried into posterity for all time. The elders and prominent personalities of our country should follow the example set by our forefathers in the glorious task of national salvation.

Rich people, soldiers, workers, peasants, intellectuals, employees, traders, youth and women who warmly love your country ! At the present time national liberation is the most important problem. Let us unite together ! As one in mind and strength we shall overthrow the Japanese and French and their jackals in order to save people from the situation between boiling water and burning heat.

Dear compatriots!

National salvation is the common cause to the whole of our people. Every Vietnamese must take a part in it. He who has money will contribute his money, he who has strength will contribute his strength, he who has talent will contribute his talent. I pledge to use all my modest abilities to follow you, and am ready for the last sacrifice.

Revolutionary fighters!

The hour has struck! Raise aloft the insurrectionary banner and guide the people throughout the country to overthrow the Japanese and French! The sacred call of the Fatherland is resounding in your ears; the blood of our heroic predecessors who sacrificed their lives is stirring in your hearts!

The fighting spirit of the people is displayed everywhere before you! Let us rise up quickly! Compatriots throughout the country, rise up quickly! Unite with each other, unify your action to overthrow the Japanese and the French.

Victory to Vietnam's Revolution!

Victory to the World's Revolution!

APPEAL FOR GENERAL INSURRECTION

(Written after the National Congress convened by the Viet Minh General Committee, August 16, 1945)

Dear compatriots,

Four years ago in one of my letters I called on you to unite together. Because unity is strength, only strength enables us to win back independence and freedom.

At present, the Japanese army is crushed. The National Salvation movement has spread to the whole country. The Revolutionary Front for the Independence of Vietnam (Viet Minh) has millions of members from all social strata: intellectuals, peasants, workers, businessmen, soldiers, and from all nationalities in the country: Kinh, Tho, Nung, Muong, Man, etc. In the Front our compatriots march side by side without discrimination as to age, sex, religion or fortune.

Recently, the Viet Minh Front convened the Vietnam People's Congress and appointed the National Liberation Committee to lead the entire people in the resolute struggle until national independence is won.

This is a great advance in the history of the struggle waged for nearly a century by our people for their liberation.

This is a fact that rejoices our compatriots and fills me with great joy.

However, we cannot consider this as good enough. Our struggle will be a long and hard one. Because the Japanese are defeated, we shall not be liberated overnight. We still have to make further efforts and carry on the struggle. Only a united struggle will bring us independence.

The Viet Minh Front is at present the basis of the struggle and solidarity of our people. Join the Viet Minh Front, support it, make it greater and stronger!

At present, the National Liberation Committee is so to speak in itself our provisional government. Unite around it and see to it that its policies and orders are carried out throughout the country!

In this way, our Fatherland will certainly win independence and our people will certainly win freedom soon.

Dear compatriots,

The decisive hour in the destiny of our people has struck. Let us stand up with all our strength to free ourselves!

Many oppressed peoples the world over are vying with each other in the march to win back their independence. We cannot allow ourselves to lag behind.

Forward! Forward! Under the banner of the Viet Minh Front, move forward courageously!

(November, 1945)

Compatriots!

During the Second World War, the French colonialists
twice sold out our country to the Japanese. Thus they betrayed the allied nations, and helped the Japanese to cause
the latter many losses.

Meanwhile they also betrayed our people, exposing us to
the destruction of bombs and bullets. In this way, the French
colonialists withdrew of their own accord from the Allied
ranks and tore up the treaties they had earlier compelled us
to sign.

Notwithstanding the French colonialists' treachery, our
people as a whole were determined to side with the Allies
and oppose the invaders. When the Japanese surrendered,
our entire people singlemindedly changed our country into
a Democratic Republic and elected a provisional Government which is to prepare for a National Congress and draw
up our draft Constitution.

Not only is our act in line with the Atlantic and San
Francisco Charters, solemnly proclaimed by the Allies, but
it entirely conforms with the glorious principles upheld by
the French people, viz. Liberty, Equality and Fraternity.

It is thus clear that in the past the colonialists betrayed
the Allies and our country, and surrendered to the Japanese.
At present, in the shadow of the British and Indian troops,
and behind the Japanese soldiers, they are attacking the
South of our country.

They have sabotaged the peace that China, the United
States, Britain and Russia won at the cost of scores of mil-

34

lions of lives. They have violated the promises concerning democracy and liberty that the Allied Powers proclaimed. They have of their own accord sabotaged their fathers' principles of liberty and equality. In consequence, it is for a just cause, for justice of the world, and for Vietnam's land and people that our compatriots throughout the country have risen to struggle, and are firmly determined to maintain their independence. We do not hate the French people and France. We are energetically fighting slavery and the ruthless policy of the French colonialists. We are not invading another's country. We only safeguard our own against the French invaders. Hence we are not alone. The countries which love peace and democracy, and the weaker nations all over the world, all sympathize with us. With the unity of the whole people within the country, and with so many sympathizers abroad, we are sure of victory.

The French colonialists have behaved lawlessly in the South for almost one and a half months. Our southern compatriots have sacrificed their lives in a most valiant struggle. Public opinion in the great countries: China, the United States, Russia and Britain, has supported our just cause.

Compatriots throughout the country ! Those in the South will do their utmost to resist the enemy. Those in the Centre and the North will endeavour to help their southern compatriots, and be on the alert.

The French colonialists should know that the Vietnamese people do not want bloodshed, that they love peace. But we are determined to sacrifice even millions of combatants, and fight a long-term war of resistance in order to safeguard Vietnam's independence and free her children from slavery. We are sure that our war of resistance will be victorious !

Let the whole country be determined in the war of resistance !

Long live independent Vietnam !

MESSAGE TO THE VIETNAMESE PEOPLE, THE FRENCH PEOPLE AND THE PEOPLES OF THE ALLIED NATIONS

(December 21, 1946)

We, the Vietnamese Government and people, are determined to struggle for our independence and national unification, but we are also ready for friendly co-operation with the French people. We therefore signed a preliminary Agreement on March 6, 1946 and for the Modus Vivendi on September 14, 1946.

But the French reactionary colonialists regard those agreements as mere scraps of paper.

In the South they continue to arrest, massacre and provoke the Vietnamese patriots. They oppress honest Frenchmen, and have set up a puppet Government in order to divide our people.

In the southern part of Central Vietnam they continue to terrorize our compatriots, attack the Vietnamese army and invade our territory.

In the North, they provoke clashes to occupy Bac Ninh, Bac Giang, Lang Son and many other localities. They blockade the port of Haiphong, thus making it impossible for the Chinese, Vietnamese, other foreigners and also French residents to carry out their business. They try to strangle the Vietnamese people and wreck our national sovereignty. At present they use tanks, aircraft, cannons and warships to massacre our compatriots, and occupy the port of Haiphong as well as other provinces lying along the rivers.

That is not all. They have gone so far as to mobilize their naval, land and air forces and send us many ultimatums. They have massacred old people, women and children in Hanoi, the capital, itself.

On December 19, 1946, at 8 p.m. Hanoi was attacked.

The French colonialists' actions aimed at invading our country are glaring and undeniable.

The Vietnamese people are now facing two alternatives: either to stay with hands bound and heads bowed as slaves again, or to struggle to the end to win back freedom and independence.

No ! The Vietnamese people cannot accept foreign domination being imposed on them again.

No ! The Vietnamese people never want to be enslaved again. They would rather die than lose their independence and freedom.

French people !

We have affection for you and sincerely want to cooperate with you within the framework of the French Union because we have a common ideal which is freedom, equality and independence.

It is the reactionary French colonialists who have blemished France's honour and are seeking to divide us by provoking a war. As soon as France acknowledges our independence and unification and calls back home the bellicose French colonialists, friendly relations and co-operation between the peoples of Viet Nam and France will be restored immediately.

French soldiers !

There is no grudge or rancour between us. It is for the sake of their selfish interests that the reactionary colonialists provoke clashes. Profits will be theirs, death yours, and medals of victory will be conferred on the militarists. But for you and your families, there is only suffering and poverty. Think it over and think again. Can you be content with sacrificing your bones and blood and your lives for the reactionaries? In joining us you will be treated as friends.

Peoples of the Allied powers !

After the recent World War, peace was restored by the democratic countries. However, the French reactionaries trampled underfoot the Atlantic and San Francisco Charters. They are waging an aggressive war in Vietnam. They must bear the whole responsibility. The Vietnamese people ask you to intervene.

Compatriots!

The Resistance war will be long and fraught with sufferings. Whatever sacrifices we have to make and however long the Resistance war will last, we are determined to fight to the end, until Vietnam is completely independent and unified. We are 20 million against 100,000 colonialists. Our victory is firmly guaranteed.

On behalf of the Government of the Democratic Republic of Vietnam, I give the following orders to the Armymen, self-defence guards, militiamen and compatriots to the three parts of Vietnam:

1 — If the French troops attack us, we must fiercely counterattack them with all the weapons at our disposal. All Vietnamese people must stand up to safeguard their Fatherland.

2 — We must protect the lives and property of foreign residents and treat prisoners of war well.

3 — Those who collaborate with the enemy will be punished. Those who help and defend their country will be rewarded.

Compatriots!

The Fatherland is in danger. All of us must rise up!

Long live independent and united Vietnam!

Long live the successful Resistance War!

To the Congress of the National Committee of the Viet Minh

(Letter dated April 20, 1948)

Today the League holds its meeting — I am very sorry that I am too busy to attend it. I wish the delegates good health and the Congress good success. May I recall some experiences to the minds of the delegates?

If the Viet Minh has been successful it is thanks to its correct policies:

(a) From the beginning, the Viet Minh's home policy has been to unite the whole people and win independence for the Fatherland.

To reach this aim, the Viet Minh decided to fight both the Japanese and the French. In these circumstances, where there was only a group of comrades with no arms at all and the Japanese and French joined together to repress the patriotic movement. Some people considered this decision was a childish one. But the result showed that the Viet Minh policy was correct.

(b) The foreign policy of the Viet Minh was to side with the democratic camp.

When the German, Italian and Japanese fascists ruled undisturbed and won victory upon victory, and the democratic countries were suffering bitter defeat upon defeat, such a policy was also considered foolish by some people. But at that time the Viet Minh foresaw that the democratic Allied forces would certainly win. The result also showed that the Viet Minh's policy was correct.

(c) While the Japanese and French were co-operating closely, the Viet Minh foresaw that they would betray each other, and the first would be the Japanese. Thanks to this foresight the Viet Minh had prepared a plan to turn this opportunity to advantage. The result also showed that the Viet Minh's policy was correct.

(d) From the beginning, the Viet Minh was sure of the ultimate independence of the Fatherland, therefore they worked out a plan for the establishment of a free zone which would not only be used as a resistance base but also as a place to train prospective military and administrative cadres. The result also showed that the Viet Minh's policy was correct.

(e) When the August Revolution was victorious and succeeded in seizing power, the Viet Minh decided to organize a government on a broad basis, including all the personalities in the country, to take in hand State affairs. Some people thought that the prominent personalities would not gladly cooperate with the Viet Minh. But as the Viet Minh put the interests of the Fatherland and the people first, these personalities willingly joined the Government.

(f) When it was necessary to further develop the unity of the whole people, the Viet Minh proposed and helped the organization of the Vietnam National United Front to develop rapidly and broadly, and thus the Viet Minh was further developed and consolidated.

(g) The Viet Minh's policy was to safeguard peace, but when the Resistance war broke out, the Viet Minh did its best to support the Government's policy of long Resistance. In this Resistance war, the Viet Minh foresaw that victory would certainly be ours. The past is a guarantee for the future.

In short, ever since the founding of the Viet Minh, experience has shown that all its policies were correct; these facts must be made known.

However, the Viet Minh had a shortcoming: its rapid development did not leave time to train all the cadres; that is why in many places the cadres deviated from the common policy, so much so that some cadres became corrupted.

At present, on the one hand, the Viet Minh must pay attention to the training of cadres from village level upwards.

On the other hand, cadres must criticize and examine themselves in order to be worthy of their hard but glorious task. And the members of the Viet Minh League must be the vanguard in every task in the Resistance and reconstruction of the country.

I hope that the Congress will work out practical plans to develop and consolidate the Viet Minh League on the lines of patriotic emulation.

MESSAGE TO PEASANT CADRES

(November 1949)

Our country is an agricultural one.

More than nine-tenths of our people are peasants.

More than nine-tenths of our peasants are middle, poor and landless peasants.

Fighters in the people's regular and local army, militia and guerilla forces are mostly peasants.

The production work to feed the army, the workers and office workers is carried out by the peasants.

Sabotage work to check the enemy, the repairing of roads, communications and transport is mostly done by the peasants.

In a word, the peasants constitute an extremely big force among the nation, and are a most loyal ally of the working class.

For the Resistance and national construction to be successfully achieved, for independence and reunification to be really attained, reliance should be placed on our peasant forces.

Our peasants have in store a big force, an ardent patriotism, a determination to struggle and make sacrifices.

Agitation among the peasants consists of:

— Systematically organizing the peasants.

— Closely uniting the peasants.

— Training the peasants to that they may be completely conscious of their rights and might.

— Leading the peasants to struggle earnestly for their own interest and that of their Fatherland.

— To carry out agitation among the peasants means to stir up all of them; that is, to make them clearly understand the interests of the nation and of their class, to get them to join the National Salvation Peasants' Association in great numbers in order to struggle for their objective, and actively participate in the Resistance war and national construction.

To achieve this end, peasant cadres must avoid subjectiveness, formalism and red tape.

Provincial cadres must go to districts and villages.

District cadres must go to villages and hamlets.

Cadres must go to the bases to see and hear for themselves and act accordingly. At the same time, they must think about what they do, and concentrate on their work in order to conduct on-the-spot inquiries, to help in control, and to draw and exchange experiences with a view to helping the peasants and learning from them.

In the administrative committees as well as in the leading bodies of the Peasants' Association, poor peasants and farmhands must really participate in management.

If the cadres (peasant cadres and cadres in state organs as well) strictly adhere to these principles and strictly carry them out

— Emulation in production to stave off famine,

— Emulation in learning the Vietnamese language to liquidate illiteracy,

— Emulation in assisting the army, and fostering the militia and guerilla force to annihilate the foreign aggressors,

will be successfully achieved.

LETTER TO CATHOLIC COMPATRIOTS

(December 9, 1949)

Dear Compatriots,

French invaders and puppet paratroops have dropped in Phat Diem. They have violated the Vietnamese holy land. This is very painful to me.

Moreover the French invaders falsely declared that they came at the invitation of the Catholics.

They did so with two wicked aims:

Firstly, to smear our Catholic compatriots and make people think that our Catholic compatriots are betraying their Fatherland and following the colonialists.

Secondly, to kindle an internecine war in which we, brothers, kill each other for their profit.

But the French invaders will fail, because for these last years our Catholic compatriots have been enthusiastic in joining the Resistance for national salation; because, for these last years, in many places the French invaders destroyed churches, ill-treated priests, raped nuns, massacred and plundered our Catholic compatriots as well as the non-Catholic. Therefore, though at first they sham kindness and try to lure and buy over our Catholic compatriots, the latter are determined not to be deceived.

The Government has sent troops to Phat Diem to fight the colonialist invaders in order to save our Catholic compatriots in this region from the shackles of these wicked devils.

Therefore you must endeavour to help our soldiers in every respect in order to smash the enemy and save yourselves and the country.

The French invaders' failure is certain, because everywhere in Viet Nam they are suffering heavier defeats with

44

every passing day, and in France their domestic situation is becoming more and more hopeless.

I hope that you will firmly maintain your patriotic spirit and have sufficient strength to oppose the French invaders in order to fulfil your sacred duty which is:

To serve God

To serve the Fatherland.

POLITICAL REPORT AT THE SECOND NATIONAL CONGRESS OF THE VIETNAM WORKERS' PARTY

(Extract from Report delivered in February 1951)

After the outbreak of World War Two, the Party Central Committee held the November 1939 session and worked out its policies: To set up a united front against the French colonialists and the imperialist war and to prepare for an insurrection. To withdraw the slogan "to confiscate the landlords' land and to distribute it to the tillers" in order to draw the landlord class into the National United Front.

After France's capitulation to fascist Germany, the Japanese encroached upon French power in Indo-China and used the French colonialists as their henchmen to repress the revolution in our country.

In that period, our people launched three uprisings in Bac Son, Nam Ky and Do Luong.

In May 1941, the Party Central Committee held its Eighth Session. The main question was to make it clear that the revolution facing Vietnam was a revolution for national liberation, and to set up the Viet Minh Front. The main slogan was: "To unite the entire people, oppose the Japanese and the French and wrest back independence; to postpone the agrarian revolution." The name Vietnam Doc Lap Dong Minh (League for the Independence of Vietnam) was very clear in meaning, practical and in full keeping with the aspirations of the entire people. Besides, the simple, practical and complete programme of the Front comprises ten points, as a propaganda song relates:

ten policies are mapped out which are, first,
useful to the country, second, beneficial to
the people . . .

These ten points include matters common to the whole nation and matters arising from the struggle for the interest of workers, peasants and all strata of the population.

As a result the Viet Minh Front was warmly welcomed by the people, and thanks to the efforts made by the cadres to keep close to the people, it developed very rapidly and very strongly. As the Front developed strongly, the Party also grew up. The Party also helped the progressive intellectuals to found the Vietnam Democratic Party in order to attract young intellectuals and civil servants and to accelerate the disintegration of the pro-Japanese Dai Viet.

In the world, the Soviet Union and the Allies scored successive victories. In our country, the Japanese and the French were in conflict. Under the Party's leadership, the Viet Minh Front grew fairly strong. In this situation, the Standing Bureau of the Central Committee held its enlarged session in March 1945. The main resolution was to speed up the anti-Japanese movement and to prepare for the general insurrection. At that time, the French colonialists' power already fell into the hands of the Japanese fascists.

In May 1945, Germany capitulated. In August, Japan surrendered. The Soviet Union and the Allies won complete victory.

Early in August, the Party held its Second National Congress at Tan Trao to decide on the plan of action and to take part in the National People's Congress convened by the Viet Minh Front. The People's Congress was also held at Tan Trao in the same month.

The National People's Congress approved the plan put forth by the Viet Minh and the order for general insurrection, and elected the Vietnam National Liberation Committee which would later become the Provisional Government of our country.

Because the Party's policies were correct, and they were carried out in good time and in a flexible way, the August General Insurrection was successful.

From the August Revolution up to now.

Thanks to the clear-sighted and resolute leadership of

our Party, and the solidarity and enthusiasm of the entire people within and without the Viet Minh Front, the August Revolution was successful.

Not only the toiling classes and people but also the oppressed people in other countries can be proud that this is the first time in the revolutionary history of colonial and semi-colonial peoples in which a party, only fifteen years of age, has led the revolution to success and seized power throughout the country.

On our part, we must bear in mind that our success was due to the great victory of the Soviet Red Army which defeated fascist Japan, to the friendly assistance of international solidarity, to the close unity of our entire people and to the heroic sacrifice of our revolutionary predecessors.

Our comrades like Tran Phu, Ngo Gia Tu, Le Hong Phong, Nguyen Thi Minh Khai, Ha Huy Tap, Nguyen Van Cu, Hoang Van Thu and thousands of others, placed the interests of the Party, the revolution, their class and nation above and before everything else. They had deep confidence in the great forces and glorious future of their class and nation. They willingly sacrificed everything, even their lives, for the sake of their Party, their class and nation. They fertilized the Revolution-tree with their blood and bones and, as a result of it, the tree of Revolution has now bloomed and borne good fruit.

All of us must follow these examples of heroism and selflessness and become genuine revolutionaries.

The August Revolution overthrew the centuries-old monarchy, broke the chains of the nearly one hundred years old colonial rule, brought back power to the people and built the basis for an independent, free and happy Democratic Republic of Vietnam.

This is an extremely great change in the history of our country.

Thanks to the successful August Revolution we have become a member of the great democratic family in the world.

The August Revolution has exerted a direct and very great influence on the two brother Cambodian and Laotian nations. After the success of the August Revolution, the Cambodian and Laotian peoples also rose up against the imperialists to claim independence.

On September 2, 1945, the Government of the Democratic Republic of Vietnam declared to the world that Vietnam had the right to be independent, and put into practice democratic freedoms in the country. Mention should be made here that some comrades, members of the Vietnam National Liberation Committee who, having been elected by the National People's Congress, should have taken part in the Provisional Government, of their own accord withdrew to give the place to patriotic personalities outside the Viet Minh Front. This was a selfless, magnanimous gesture of men who did not care for position and put the interests of the nation, of the national union, above individual interests. This is a praise-worthy, honourable gesture that we must imitate.

The difficulties of the Party and Government:

As soon as the people's power came into existence it met with great difficulties.

Due to the policy of ruthless exploitation by the Japanese and the French, within only half a year (end of 1944 and beginning of 1945) more than two million people in the North died of starvation.

We were independent for hardly one month when the British troops entered the South. They allegedly came to disarm the Japanese army, but were in reality an expeditionary corps helping the French colonialists in their attempt to re-occupy our country.

The Kuomintang troops entered the North under the same pretext, but actually they had three wicked aims:

— to annihilate our Party,

— to smash the Viet Minh Front,

— to help the Vietnamese reactionaries overthrow the people's power in order to set up a reactionary government under their sway.

In the face of that grave and pressing situation, our Party did everything possible to keep itself in existence, to work and develop, to give discreet and more effective leadership in order to have the time gradually to consolidate the forces of the people's power and to strengthen the National United Front.

At that time the Party could not hesitate: hesitation meant failure. The Party had to make quick decisions and take measures — even painful ones — to save the situation. The greatest worry was about the Party's proclamation of voluntary dissolution. But in reality it went underground.

And though underground, the Party continued to lead the administration and the people.

We recognise that the Party's declaration of dissolution (actual withdrawal into the underground) was a good measure.

In spite of many a big difficulty, the Party and the Government guided our country through dangerous rapids and implemented many points in the programme of the Viet Minh Front:

— Holding the General Elections to elect the National Assembly and chart the Constitution,

— Building and consolidating the people's power,

— Annihilating the Vietnamese reactionaries,

— Building and strengthening the people's army and arming the people,

— Elaborating labour laws,

— Reducing land rent and interest rates,

— Building people's culture,

— Broadening and consolidating the national united front (setting up of the All Vietnam Union).

Mention should be made of the Preliminary Agreement of March 6, 1946, and the Modus Vivendi of September 14, 1946, because they were considered as ultra-rightist and caused much grumbling. But in the opinion of our comrades and compatriots in the South they were correct. Indeed they were, because our comrades and compatriots cleverly availed themselves of this opportunity to build up and develop their forces.

Lenin said that if even a compromise with bandits were advantageous to the revolution, he would do it.

We needed peace to build our country, and therefore we made concessions to maintain peace. Although the French colonialists broke their word and unleashed war, nearly one year of temporary peace gave us time to build up our basic forces.

When the French deliberately provoked war, we could no longer put up with them, and the nation-wide war broke out.

The long-term Resistance War:

The enemy planned a lightning war. As they wanted to attack swiftly and win swiftly, our Party and Government put forward the slogan "long-term Resistance War". The enemy plotted to sow dissension among us, so our slogan was "Unity of the entire people".

Therefore right from the start, our strategy prevailed over the enemy's.

To wage a long-term resistance war, there must be an adequate supply of arms and munitions to the army, of food and clothing to the troops and the people. Our country is poor and our technique low. The cities and towns which have some industry are occupied by the enemy. We tried to offset our material deficiencies by the enthusiasm of the entire people. So the Party and the Government promoted patriotic emulation. Emulation covers all fields but it is aimed at three main points: doing away with famine, wiping out illiteracy and annihilating the foreign invaders.

Our workers emulated in manufacturing weapons for our troops, who enthusiastically trained themselves and magnificently scored feats of arms. The recent victories were proof of this. Our people ardently emulated and got satisfactory results: our country is economically backward, we have been waging the Resistance War for four or five years and still can withstand it without suffering too many privations. This is a fact. The majority of our population are freed from illiteracy. This is a glorious achievement lauded by the world. I suggest that our Congress should send affectionate thanks and congratulations to our troops and compatriots.

But our organisation, supervision, exchange and summing up of experiences are still weak. This is our shortcoming. From now on we strive to overcome them and the emulation movement will certainly bring about many more and better results.

The military aspect is the key aspect in the Resistance war.

At the beginning of the Resistance War our army was young. Though full of heroism, it lacked weapons, experience, officers, everything.

The enemy army was well-known in the world. They had navy, infantry and air forces. Moreover they were supported by the British and American imperialists, especially by the latter.

The difference between our force and the enemy's was so great that there were at the time people who likened our Resistance war to a "locust fighting an elephant".

It was so if things were seen from the material side, in their actual conditions and with a narrow mind. We had to oppose airplanes and cannons with bamboo sticks. But guided by Marxism-Leninism our Party did not look only at the present but also at the future and had firm confidence in the spirit and force of the masses, of the nation. Therefore we resolutely told the wavering and pessimistic people that:

"Today the locust fights the elephant

"But tomorrow the elephant will be disembowelled".

Practical life has shown that the colonialist 'elephant' is being disembowelled while our army has grown up into a powerful tiger.

Although at the beginning, the enemy was the stronger and we the weaker, we doggedly waged the Resistance war, scored many successes and firmly believed in our final victory because our cause is just and our troops courageous, our people united and undaunted and because we are supported by the French people and the world democratic camp, and also because our strategy is correct.

Our Party and Government foresaw that our Resistance war has three stages:

The first stage going from September 23, 1945, to the closing of the Viet Bac campaign, in Autumn-Winter 1947, in which all we did was to preserve and increase our main forces.

The second stage running from the end of the Viet Bac campaign 1947 up to now, in which we have actively contended with the enemy and prepared for the general counter-offensive.

The third stage is the general counter-offensive.

Because they did not grasp this point of the policy of the Party and the Government, a number of comrades got wrong ideas. Some said that the slogan for general counter-offensive was put forward too early. Others wanted to know the date of the general counter-offensive. Still others believed that the general counter-offensive would certainly be launched in 1950, etc.

These wrong conceptions were harmful to our work. We must first of all keep in mind that the Resistance War will be long and hard, but we will win.

The Resistance War must be long because we have a small population and a small territory and our country is poor. Long and thorough preparations have to be made by our whole nation. We must always bear in mind that compared to us the French invaders are quite strong, and, in addition, they are assisted by the British and Americans.

They are a "thickpeel-mandarine"; we must have time to "sharpen our nails" to tear them to pieces.

We must also understand that each stage is linked up with another, the second succeeds the first and produces seeds for the third.

Many changes occur in the course of one stage to another. Each stage also has changes of its own.

It is possible to examine the general situation in order to divide it into big stages, but it is not possible to cut off completely one stage from the other like cutting bread. The length of each stage depends on the situation in the home country and in the world, and on the changes between the enemy forces and ours. We must understand that the long-term Resistance war is closely connected with the preparations for general counter-offensive. As the Resistance war is long there must also be long preparation for the general counter-offensive. It depends on the changes between the enemy forces and ours, and also on the changes in the international situation whether the general counter-offensive will come early or late.

In all circumstances, the more careful and complete the preparation, the more favourable will be the general counter-offensive and the more certain our success.

The slogan "To prepare strongly for the general counter-offensive" was put forward early in 1950.

Did we make preparations during that year?

Yes, we did. The Government issued the general mobilisation order and launched the movement for patriotic emulation. As is well-known, the troops and the people have been striving to make preparations and have obtained good results.

Did we pass to the general counter-offensive in 1950?

Yes, we did and are passing to it. The big diplomatic successes scored early in 1950 and the victories won on the battlefronts at the end of that year were proof of this.

Have we launched the general counter-offensive?

We have been preparing to switch over to the general counter-offensive which is not yet actually being carried out. We must fully grasp the meaning of the words, "to prepare to pass strongly over to . . ."

Once the preparations are complete we will launch the general counter-offensive. The more complete the prepar ations, the quicker will come the hour for launching the general counter-offensive and the more favourable will it be.

We should avoid precipitation, rashness and impatience.

The troops, the people, the cadres, everybody and every sector must strive to make complete preparations. When our preparations are completed we will launch the general counter-offensive and it will certainly be successful.

MESSAGE TO PUPPET TROOPS

(Leaflet, 1951)

VIETNAMESE SERVING IN THE FRENCH ARMY AND PUPPET ARMY!

Once again, the French want to invade our country. They dish out a false independence to delude our people and pressgang you into their armies.

The puppet Bao Dai sold out our country to the French as his ancestors surrendered to them throughout eighty years. He used our compatriots as cannon fodder for the French.

To serve in the French army and the puppet troops is to help them kill our compatriots and to stand against the Fatherland.

Our Government and people wage the Resistance war to regain genuine independence for the Fatherland and secure genuine freedom for our people. Therefore, the forces of the Resistance are growing with every passing day and our Resistance will certainly be victorious.

I know that you are Vietnam's children and that you are coerced or deluded by the enemy into their armies, while nobody among you wishes to "carry the snake to kill our poultry", "to bring the elephant home to trample on the tombs of our ancestors", to stand against the Fatherland and to be called traitors.

In the recent battles, many among you have passed over to the side of our Government.

Those who carried guns and ammunition with them were rewarded by the Government.

Those who desired to return to their native villages were helped by the Government to do so.

Those who wished to fight the enemy, to perform military deeds, were authorised to enlist in our army.

I earnestly call on you all to immediately pass over to the side of the Fatherland: you will be welcomed.

Like red silk covering a mirror.

Children of the same Hong Lac ancestors! Let us love one another.

PREFACE TO THE TRANSLATION OF THE BOOK "THE UNDER-
GROUND PARTY COMMITTEE" BY FEDOROV

(1951)

This is the first time I have prefaced a book, because this
book appears in the nick of time — just when we are intensifying the guerilla movement.

Experiences learnt in the Soviet Union, in China and in
our country have demonstrated that the guerilla movement
is a force of paramount importance for a war for national
liberation. On a powerful guerilla force depends the victory
of a war of liberation.

A close and widespread guerilla network set up in and
around enemy controlled areas, in all villages, districts and
provinces, is an iron net which can enmesh the enemy without giving him a chance of escaping. The enemy can be
attacked wherever he goes. Everything done by him can be
destroyed. He is blind, deaf and maimed even if he has eyes,
ears and limbs. Part of the enemies can be killed piecemeal;
those who are alive are nervous, afraid even of the whine of
the wind and the chirpings of birds, and will finally be wiped
out by the guerillas.

A skilful guerilla organisation makes it possible for people
of all walks of life — men and women, old and young, intellectuals, peasants, workers, traders, etc. — to take part in all
activities: fighting the enemy, supplies, reconnaissance,
liaison, propaganda, etc. In short everyone has a chance of
serving his Fatherland.

To attain this goal, the following points are necessary:
— The Party and Government will strengthen their
leadership of the guerilla movement:
— The cadres and people at large must be clearsighted;
they must firmly believe·in the Party and Government

57

policies, in the people's strength and in the final victory of our country;

— The cadres must establish close relations with the people; they must win their confidence, esteem and love;

— The people must have a great patriotism and be ready to sacrifice themselves for the Fatherland, for the happiness and future of the country.

We have the people as the mainstay, let us consolidate it. We have cadres, let us train and foster them. We have the guerilla movement, let us develop it. The lessons learnt from the guerilla movement in the Soviet Union will be helpful to us. Certainly we shall succeed in our work of pushing forward the guerilla movement.

THE IMPERIALIST AGRESSORS CAN NEVER ENSLAVE THE HEROIC VIETNAMESE PEOPLE

(Extracts from article in the journal "For a Lasting Peace, for a People's Democracy", Bucharest, April 4, 1952.)

COLLUSION BETWEEN THE AGRESSORS

Let us review Viet Nam's situation in 1951.

After their defeat in the China-Viet Nam border campaign in October 1950 — the greatest reverse they had ever suffered in the whole history of their colonial wars, which involved for them the loss of five provinces at one time — Cao Bang, Lang Son, Lao Cai, Thai Nguyen and Hoa Binh — the French colonialists began the year 1951 with the despatch of General de Lattre de Tassigny to Viet Nam.

They resorted to total war. Their manoeuvre was to consolidate the Bao Dai puppet government, organise puppet troops and redouble spying activities. They set up no man's lands of from 5 to 10 kilometres wide around areas under their control and strengthened the Red River delta by a network of 2,300 bunkers. They stepped up mopping-up operations in our rear, applied the policy of annihilation and wholesale destruction of our manpower and potential resources by killing our compatriots, devastating our countryside, burning our ricefields, etc. In a word, they followed the policy of "using Vietnamese to fight Vietnamese and nursing the war by means of warfare".

It is on the orders and with the assistance of their masters, the American interventionists, that the French colonialists performed the above-mentioned deeds.

Among the first Americans now living in Vietnam (of course in areas under French control) there is a fairly well-known spy, Donald Heath, ambassador accredited to the puppet government and a general, head of the U.S. military mission.

In September 1951, de Lattre de Tassigny went to Washington to make his report and beg for aid.

In October, General Collins, Chief of Staff of the U.S. Army, came to Vietnam to inspect the French Expeditionary Corps and puppet troops.

In order to show their American masters that U.S. aid is used in a worthwhile manner at present as well as in the future, in November de Lattre de Tassigny attacked the chief town of Hoa Binh province. The result of this "shooting offensive" which the reactionary press in France and in the world commented on enthusiastically, was that the Vietnam People's Army caught the overwhelming majority of enemy troops tightly between two prongs and annihilated them. But this did not prevent de Lattre de Tassigny and his henchmen from claiming that they had carried the day!

From the very beginning of the war, the Americans supplied France with money and armaments. To take an example, 85 per cent of weapons, war materials and even canned food captured by our troops were labelled "made in U.S.A." This aid was stepped up all the more rapidly since June 1950 when the U.S.A. began interfering in Korea. American aid to the French invaders consisted of airplanes, boats, trucks, military outfits, napalm bombs, etc.

Meanwhile, the Americans compelled the French colonialists to step up the organisation of four divisions of puppet troops, with each party footing half the bill. Of course, this collusion between the French and American aggressors and the puppet clique was fraught with contradictions and contentions.

The French colonialists are now landed in a dilemma: either they receive U.S. aid and are then replaced by their American "allies", or they receive nothing, and are then defeated by the Vietnamese people. To organise the puppet army by means of pressganging the youth in areas under their control would be tantamount to swallowing a bomb when one is hungry: a day will come when at last the bomb bursts inside. However, not to organise the army on this basis would mean instantaneous death for the enemy because even the French strategists have to admit that the French Expeditionary Corps grows thinner and thinner and is on the verge of collapse.

Furthermore, U.S. aid is paid for at a very high price. In the enemy-held areas, French capitalism is swept aside by American capitalism. American concerns like the Petroleum Oil Corporation, the Caltex Oil Corporation, the Bethlem Steel Corporation, the Florid Phosphate Corporation and others, monopolise rubber, ores, and other natural resources of our country. U.S. goods swamp the market. The French reactionary press, especially Le Monde, is compelled to acknowledge sadly that French capitalism is now giving way to U.S. capitalism.

The U.S. interventionists have nurtured the French aggressors and the Vietnamese puppets, but the Vietnamese people do not let anybody delude and enslave them.

People's China is our close neighbour. Her brilliant example gives us a great impetus. Not long ago the Chinese people defeated the U.S. imperialists and won an historical victory. The execrated Chiang Kai-shek was swept from the Chinese mainland, though he is more cunning than the placeman Bao Dai. Can the U.S. interventionists, who were drummed out of China and are now suffering heavy defeats in Korea, conquer Vietnam? Of course not!

ACHIEVEMENTS RECORDED BY THE DEMOCRATIC REPUBLIC OF VIET NAM

In 1951, the Vietnamese people made a big stride forward. In the political field, the founding of the Vietnam Workers' Party, the amalgamation of the Viet Minh and Lien Viet, the setting up of the Committee of action for Vietnam, Cambodia and Laos, greatly consolidated the unity and enhanced the cofidence of the Vietnamese people; they strengthened the alliance between the three brother countries in their struggle against the common enemies — the French colonialists and U.S. interventionists — in order to realise their common goal, i.e. national independence.

So we were able to frustrate the enemy's policy of "Divide and rule".

In the economic field, the National Bank of Vietnam has been established, our finance is placed under centralised and unified supervision, and communications have been reorganised.

Formerly we demolished roads to check the enemy's advance; at present we repair them to drive the enemy to an early defeat. Formerly we did our utmost to sabotage roads, now we encounter great difficulties in mending them, but have managed to complete our work quite rapidly. This is a hard job, especially when we lack machines. However, thanks to the enthusiasm and sacrificing spirit of our people, this work was carried through. To avoid enemy air raids, it was done at night by workers even knee deep in water. In the bright torch light, hundreds of men, women and young people dug the earth to fill the gaps in the roads, broke stones, felled trees and built bridges. As in any other work, here the workers' enthusiasm was roused by emulation drives. I am sure that you would be astonished to see teams of old volunteers from 60 to 80 years competing with teams of young workers.

Here it must be pointed out that in the free zone most of the work is done at night — children go to school, housewives go to market and guerillas go to attack the enemy . . .

Great successes have been achieved in the elaboration of the agricultural tax. Formerly the peasants were compelled to pay taxes of various kinds and make many other contributions; nowadays, they have only to pay a uniform tax in kind. Households whose production does not exceed 60 kilogrammes of paddy per year are exempt from tax. Households who harvest greater quantities have to pay a graduated tax. Generally speaking, the taxes to be paid do not exceed 20 per cent of the total value of the annual production. To collect taxes in time, the Party, the National United

Front and the Government have mobilised a great number of cadres to examine the new tax from the political and technical points of view. After their study, these cadres go to the countryside and hold talks and meetings to exchange views with the peasants and explain to them the new taxation policy.

After this preparatory period, the peasants of both sexes appoint a committee composed of representatives of the administration and various peoples' organisations whose duty it is to estimate the production of each household and fix the rate to be paid after approval by a Congress in which all the peasants take part.

This reform was welcomed by the population who enthusiastically took part in this tax collection.

Agricultural tax has been established simultaneously with the movement for increased production. At present the Government possesses adequate stocks of foodstuffs to cater for the soldiers and workers.

So we have thwarted the enemy's cunning plot of blockading us to reduce us to starvation.

As far as mass education is concerned, in 1951 we scored worthwhile results. Though great difficulties were created by the war, such as frequent changes of school site, schooling at night time, lack of school requisites, the number of schools rose from 2,712 in 1950 to 3,591 in 1951 with an attendance of 293,256 and 411,098 pupils respectively.

In South Vietnam the situation is all the more ticklish. There, the free zones exist everywhere, but they are not safe. Children go to their class-rooms — in fact there are only single class-rooms and not schools in the strict meaning of this word — with the same vigilance as their fathers and brothers display in guerilla fighting. Despite that, at present there are in South Vietnam 3,332 class-rooms attended by 111,700 pupils.

The liquidation of illiteracy is actively undertaken. In the first half of 1951, there were in zone III, zone V and Viet Bac zone, 324,000 people who were freed from illiteracy and 350,000 others who began learning. During the same period illiteracy was wiped out in 53 villages and 3 districts (one district is composed of from 5 to 10 villages).

People's organisations opened 837 classes attended by 9,800 public employees.

The Party, National United Front, Government, the General Confederation of Labour and the Army have periodically opened short term political training courses (about one week).

In short, great efforts are being made in mass education.

COMPLETE FAILURE OF THE FRENCH COLONIALISTS

As soon as de Lattre de Tassigny set foot in Vietnam early in 1951, he boasted of the eventual victories of the French troops.

After his defeat and disillusion at the beginning of 1952 he realised that he would soon meet with complete failure.

The fate of the French colonialists' policy brought misgivings to the most reactionary circles in France.

In the paper *Information* issued on October 22, 1951, Daladier, one of the "criminals" in the Munich affair, wrote, "Delving into the real reason of our desperate financial situation, we shall see that one of the underlying causes was lack of ripe consideration of our policy over Indo-China ... In 1951, an expenditure of as much as 330,000 million francs was officially reserved for the Indo-Chinese budget. Due to the constant rise in the prices of commodities and increase in the establishments of the French Expeditionary Corps which number 180,000 at present, it should be expected that in 1952 this expenditure will increase by 100,000 million francs. We have the impression that the war in Indo-China has caused exceedingly grave danger to our financial as well as military situation ... It is impossible to foresee a rapid victory in a war which has lasted five years and is in many ways reminiscent of the war unleashed by Napoleon against Spain and the expedition against Mexico during the Second Empire".

In its issue of December 13, 1951, the paper *Intrasigeant* wrote, "France is paralysed by the war in Indo-China. We have gradually lost the initiative of operation because our main forces are now pinned down in the plains of north Viet Nam ... In 1951, 330,000 million francs were earmarked for the military budget of Indo-China, while according to the official figures, our expenditure amounted to over 350,000 million. A credit of 380,000 million francs will be allotted to the 1952 budget but in all probability the mark of 500,000 million will be reached. Such is the truth ... Whenever France tried to take some action, well, she immediately realised that she was paralysed by the war in Indo-China".

In its number of December 16, 1951, *Franc Tireur* wrote, "General Vo Nguyen Giap's battalions, which are said to have been annihilated and to have a shattered morale, are now launching counter-offensives in the Hanoi region ... It is more and more obvious that the policy we have followed up to the present time has failed. Today it is clear that it has met with complete failure".

Hereunder is an excerpt from a letter sent to his colleagues by Captain Gazignoff, of the French Expeditionary Corps, captured by us on January 7, 1952 in the Hoa Binh battle. "Taken prisoner a few days ago, I am very astonished at the kind and correct attitude of the Vietnam People's armymen towards me ... The Vietnamese troops will certainly win final victory, because they struggle for a noble ideal, a common cause, and are swayed by a self-imposed discipline. It is as clear as daylight that the Vietnam People's Army will crush the French Expeditionary Corps, but it is ready to receive any of us who will pass over to its side.

"French officers, non-commissioned officers and men who want to go over to the Vietnam People's Army will be considered as friends and will be set free".

THE VIETNAMESE PEOPLE WILL WIN

In 1952, Vietnam will embark on a programme which includes the following points:

— To buckle down to production work and consolidate the national economy,

— To struggle and annihilate the enemy's forces. To intensify guerilla warfare,

— To expose by all means the enemy's policy of "using the Vietnamese to fight the Vietnamese, and nursing the war by means of warfare".

— To closely link patriotism to internationalism,

— Energetically to combat bureaucracy, corruption and waste.

The patriotism and heroism of the Vietnamese people allow us to have firm confidence in final victory.

The Vietnamese people's future is as bright as the sun in spring. Overjoyed at the radiance of the sun in spring, we shall struggle for the splendid future of Vietnam, for the future of democracy, world peace and socialism. We triumph at the present time, we shall triumph in the future, because our path is enlightened by the great teachings of Marxism—Leninism.

OPPOSE CORRUPTION

(extract from statement published in 1952)

To wage a revolution is to annihilate what is bad, and build what is good. We wage our revolution to annihilate the colonial and feudal regime and build a new democracy.

Though the colonialists and feudalists are annihilated, the evils left by them still exist; our revolutionary work is, therefore, not yet completed, because these evils still undermine and sabotage the constructive work of the Revolution.

There are persons who are enthusiastic, faithful in struggle; they neither flinch from dangers, hardships, nor fear the enemy, thus they *render services to the revolution;* but when they have some power in hand, unconsciously they become proud, luxurious, indulge in corruption, waste, and are bureaucratic, *and thus they do harm to the revolution.* We must save them, help them restore their revolutionary virtues. Some people say they serve the Fatherland and the people, but in the material point of view they fall easily into corruption and waste, and harm the Fatherland and the people. We must educate them, and lead them to the revolutionary path.

Corruption, waste, and bureaucracy are the evils left by the old society. They spring from self-interestedness and selfishness, and from the regime of "exploitation of man by man".

We want to build a *new society*, a free society where all men are equal, a society where industriousness, thrift, integrity and righteousness prevail, hence we must wipe out all the bad habits of the old society.

The armymen do not hesitate to sacrifice their lives and our compatriots do not spare their sweat to save the country.

The fighters devote their lives, our compatriots their work and wealth to the Government and the Party to wage the Resistance war and reconstruct the country. This is also a form of *democratic centralism*.

The Government and the Party entrust the officers with the right of commanding the armymen, and make use of money in the Resistance war and national reconstruction. The duty of the cadres is to take care of and love every fighter, value and save every cent, every bowl of rice, every work hour of their compatriots. At the same time the fighters and compatriots have the right to oblige the cadres to fulfil this task, and the right to criticise those who do not fulfil it.

Democracy is to rely on the force of the masses, to correctly follow the mass line. Hence, to be successful, the movement against corruption, waste and bureaucracy must rely on the force of the masses.

By the masses we mean all the armymen, all the workers in the factories, all civil-servants in the public services, etc., and the entire people. As in any other work, *only by mobilising the masses, implementing democracy*, making the masses understand and participate enthusiastically in this movement, shall we be certain of succeeding. The greater the participation of the masses, the more complete and rapid the achievements.

The task of the masses is to participate enthusiastically in the movement against corruption, waste and bureaucracy. The fighters contribute their labour, and the people their wealth to fight the enemy, and save the country. Corruption, waste and bureaucracy are a kind of "internal enemy". If the fighters and the people strive to oppose the enemy from outside, and forget to fight the enemy inside, they do not fulfil their task. Therefore they must participate enthusiastically in this movement.

From the highest level downwards we must as one man unite our forces to succeed in this movement. This success will help us strengthen our solidarity and further raise productivity. It helps our cadres transform their ideology, heighten their consciousness, become permeated with revolutionary virtues, and enthusiastically serve the armymen and the people. It helps purify our power and makes it worthy of the fighters' and compatriots' confidence and sacrifice. It will help us fulfil the plan of the Government and the Party to increase production and practise thrift, and fully prepare for the shifting to the general counter-offensive.

REPLIES TO A SWEDISH CORRESPONDENT

(November, 1953)

Question: The debate in the French National Assembly has proved that a great number of French politicians are for a peaceful settlement of the conflict in Vietnam by direct negotiations with the Vietnamese Government. This desire is spreading among the French people. Does your Government ando you welcome it?

Answer: The war in Vietnam was launched by the French Government. The Vietnamese people are obliged to take up arms and have heroically struggled for nearly eight years against the aggressors, to safeguard our independence and the right to live freely and peacefully. Now, if the French colonialists continue their aggressive war, the Vietnamese people are determined to carry on the patriotic resistance until final victory. However, if the French Government has drawn a lesson from the war they have been waging these last years and want to negotiate an armistice in Vietnam and to solve the Vietnam problem by peaceful means, the people and Government of the Democratic Republic of Vietnam are ready to meet this desire.

Question: Will a cease fire or an armistice be possible?

Answer: A cessation of hostilities is possible, provided that the French Government ends its war of aggression in Vietnam. The French government's sincere respect for the genuine independence of Vietnam must be the basis of the armistie.

Question: Would you agree to a neutral country mediating to organise a meeting between you and the representatives of the High Command of the other side? May Sweden be entrusted with this responsibility?

Answer: If there are neutral countries who try to speed up a cessation of hostilities in Viet Nam by means of negotiations, they will be welcomed. However, the negotiation for an armistice is mainly a concern of the Government of the Democratic Republic of Vietnam and the French Government.

Question: In your opinion, is there any other way to end the hostilities?

Answer: The war in Vietnam has brought havoc to the Vietnamese people and at the same time caused countless sufferings to the French people, therefore the French people are struggling against the war in Vietnam.

I have constantly showed my sympathy, affection and respect for the French people and the French peace fighters. Today not only is the independence of Vietnam seriously jeopardised but the independence of France is also gravely threatened. On the one hand, the U.S. imperialists egg on the French colonialists to continue and expand the aggressive war in Vietnam, thus weakening them more and more through fighting in the hope of replacing France in Indo-China; on the other, they oblige France to ratify the European defence treaty that is to revive German militarism.

Therefore the struggle of the French people to gain independence, democracy and peace for France and to end the war in Vietnam, constitutes one of the important factors to settle the Vietnam question by peaceful means.

November 26, 1953

LAND REFORM

(extract from Report to the National Assembly of the Democratic Republic of Vietnam, December, 1953.)

Our revolution is a people's national democratic revolution against aggressive imperialism and its mainstay, feudalism.

Our slogan during the Resistance war is "All for the front, al for victory!" The more the Resistance war develops, the more manpower and wealth it requires and our peasants have contributed the greatest part of manpower and wealth to the Resistance. We must liberate them from the feudal yoke, foster them in order fully to mobilise this huge force for the Resistance to win victory.

The key to the victory of the Resistance lies in consolidating and enlarging the National United Front, consolidating the worker-peasant alliance and the people's power, strengthening and developing the Army, consolidating the Party and strengthening its leadership in all aspects. Only by mobilising the masses to carry out land reform can we carry out these works satisfactorily.

The enemy actively uses Vietnamese to fight Vietnamese and feeds war by war. They are doing their utmost to deceive, divide and exploit our people. Land reform will exert an influence on and encourage our peasant compatriots in the enemy rear to struggle more enthusiastically against the enemy, in order to liberate themselves and more enthusiastically to support the Democratic Resistance Government; at the same time it exerts an influence on and disintegrates the puppet army because the absolute majority of the puppet soldiers are peasants in enemy occupied areas.

The absolute majority of our people are peasants. Over these last years, thanks to their forces, the Resistance war has been successful. In the future, it is also thanks to the peasant forces that we will be able to gain complete victory and successfully build our country.

Our peasants account for almost 90 per cent of the population but they own only 30 per cent of the arable land, and have to work hard all the year round and suffer poverty all their lives.

The landlord and feudal class accounts for less than 5 per cent of the population but they and the colonialists occupy about 70 per cent of the arable land, live in clover and do nothing. This situation is most unjust. Our country has been invaded, our people are backward and poor. During the Resistance years though the Government has carried out the policy of land rent reduction, land rent refunding and temporary distribution of land (belonging to the French and Vietnamese traitors) and communal land to the peasants in the free areas; the key problem which is not yet solved is that the peasant masses do not have land or lack land. This exerts an influence on the peasant forces in the Resistance war and production.

Only by implementing land reform, giving land to the tillers, liberating the productive forces in the countryside from the feudal yoke can we do away with poverty and backwardness, strongly mobilise the huge forces of the peasants to develop production and speed up the Resistance war to complete victory.

The goal set for land reform is to wipe out the feudal system of land appropriation, distribute land to the tillers, liberate the productive forces in the countryside, develop production and speed up the Resistance war.

The general line and policy is entirely to rely on landless and land poor peasants, closely to unite with the middle peasants, to rally with the rich peasants, to wipe out feudal exploitation step by step and with differentiation, to develop production, and to speed up the Resistance war.

To conform to the characteristics of the Resistance war and of the National United Front, which are to meet the needs of the peasants in land, at the same time to consolidate and develop the National United Front in a way favourable to the Resistance war and to production, while implementing land reform, we must apply different kinds of treatment to the landlords according to the political attitude of each of them. This means that we must apply a policy of differentiation which consists in confiscation, requisitioning with or without compensation. We will not apply a policy of wholesale confiscation or wholesale requisitioning without compensation.

The guiding principle for land reform is to boldly mobilise the peasants, to rely on the masses, correctly to follow the main line, to organise, educate and lead the peasants to struggle in a planned way, step by step, according to a proper order and under close leadership.

The dispersion of land by landlords after the promulgation of the land rent reduction decree (July 14, 1949) is illegal (except for particular cases dealt with in the Circular issued by the Prime Minister's Office on June 1, 1959).

The land confiscated or requisitioned with or without compensation is to be distributed to the peasants who have no land or are short of it. The peasants have the right to ownership of the land thus distributed.

The guiding principle for land distribution is to take villages as units, to allot land to those who previously tilled it, to take into consideration the quantity, quality and situation of the land, to give a greater share of land to those who do not have enough, to give fertile land to those who have poor land, to give land which is situated only near the village to those who have only land situated far from their houses, to give priority to the peasants who previously tilled the land to be distributed.

The die-hard elements who are determined to sabotage land reform and the traitors, reactionaries, despots who are sentenced to 5 years imprisonment upwards will not receive land.

The mass mobilisations launched this year are for experimental purposes and for the preparation for the land reform next year. These experimental drives have given us a number of experiences. In general, in the localities where the Party and Government policies have been firmly grasped and the mass line correctly followed (except in some localities where a number of cadres have committed mistakes and deviations) satisfactory results have been scored.

The mass mobilisation has failed in localities where it was launched hurriedly by impatient local cadres without the decision of the Central authorities.

Land reform is a policy applied throughout the country, but it must be carried out step by step, first in localities where sufficient conditions have been obtained and then in other localities.

After the land reform law is approved by the National Assembly, the Government will, next year, fix the date and the localities in the free zone in which land reform will be carried out.

The Government will deal with the regions inhabited by the national minorities, the Fifth zone, south Vietnam and the guerilla bases later on. In guerilla and enemy occupied areas land reform will be carried out after their liberation.

In the localities where the mass mobilisation is not yet launched for radical land-rent reduction, we have to wait until it is completed before carrying out land reform. We must do so in order to organise the peasants, raise their political consciousness, build their political supremacy in the villages, at the same time to train cadres, readjust the organisation, prepare political conditions for land reform.

No locality is allowed to start the mass mobilisation for land reform without the decision of the Government.

Land reform is a peasant revolution, a class struggle in the countryside; it is a large-scale, hard and complicated struggle, that is why preparations must be carefully made, plans clearly mapped out, the leadership very tight, the localities judiciously chosen, the time strictly followed and the implementation correct. These are conditions leading to success.

The experiences of other countries have taught us that a successful land reform will help us overcome many difficulties and solve many problems.

In the military field, our peasant compatriots will take part in the Resistance war more enthusiastically, thus helping the development of the Army and the mobilisation of the people for voluntary labour to serve the Resistance. Our soldiers will have less worry about their families and will fight more fiercely.

In the political field the political and economic power in the countryside will be in the hands of the peasants, the people's democratic dictatorship will be carried out genuinely, the worker-peasant alliance will be firmer, the National United Front will include more than 90 per cent of the people in the countryside and will become prodigiously great and strong.

In the economic field, liberated from feudalism and landlordism the peasants will joyfully carry out production and practise thrift, consumption will be increased, industry and commerce will develop and the national economy as a whole will expand.

Thanks to the development of production, the livelihood of the peasants, workers, soldiers and cadres will be improved more rapidly.

In culture and social welfare, the large majority of the people will have enough food and clothes (as the saying goes, "one must eat to be able to discharge one's duty"), they will study more enthusiastically, thereby good customs will develop. The experiences drawn from the localities where the mass mobilisation was launched show that our compatriots are very fond of study. This is a good opportunity for the intellectuals to serve the people.

As is said above, land reform is a widespread, complicated and hard class struggle. It is all the more complicated and all the harder because we are conducting the Resistance war. But it is just because we want to speed up the Resistance war to victory that we must be determined to make land reform a success. It is a complicated and hard struggle, that is why a number of cadres (Party members or non-Party members) may commit mistakes and deviations in their thinking, in their action and in implementing the policies on land reform. To prevent and put right these shortcomings and mistakes, we must firmly grasp the policies of the Party and Government, completely rely on the masses and correctly follow the mass line.

The Government and the Party call on all the cadres and Party members correctly to abide by the policies of the Government and the Party, to keep discipline, to side entirely with the peasants, to lead them in their struggle, to sacrifice their private interests for the interests of the Resistance war and of the masses when there are contradictions between their private interests and the interests of the Resistance war and of the peasant masses.

We must mobilise the entire Party, entire Army and entire people to ensure the implementation of land reform, to fulfill this great task.

With regard to the members and cadres of various democratic parties and to patriotic personalities, this is an enormous trial. We must all win the battle in this trial, as we are winning the battle in the immense trial which is the Resistance war against aggressive imperialism.

That is why our two central tasks in the next years are to do our utmost to fight the enemy and to carry out land reform.

We must strive to fight the enemy on various fronts, to annihilate the enemy forces as much as possible, to smash his new military schemes.

We must mobilise the masses to carry out land reform in the localities fixed by the Government.

To carry out land reform is to secure victory for the Resistance war.

To fight this enemy, to annihilate the enemy forces is to secure succes for land reform.

All other works must be subordinated to those two central tasks and serve them. In 1954, we must pay particular importance to three great works:

To combine land reform with the strengthening of the armed forces (the regular army, the local army, the militia and guerilla units) in all aspects: organisation, training, raising of their political and technical level and their combativeness.

To combine land reform with the training of cadres and raising their ideology, and with the promoting and readjustment of cadres, the readjustment of the Party bases in the countryside.

To combine land reform with the development of agricultural production, to ensure the requirements of the Resistance war and food for the people, in order to push forward the activities of the national economy.

Fully to implement these two central tasks and three great works is to create more favourable conditions for the carrying out of other works, such as firmly to maintain and develop the struggle in the enemy rear, to consolidate the people's democratic power in the villages, to reorganise the security service, to develop and consolidate the National United Front, to collect agricultural taxes, to develop economy and finance, and to intensify propaganda, develop education, culture and social welfare.

Our forces lie in millions of peasants who are ready to wait for the Government and Party to organise and lead them in order enthusiastically to rise up and smash the feudal and colonial yoke. With skilful organisation and leadership, these forces will shake heaven and earth, all the colonialists and feudalists will be swept away. We can conclude that under the correct leadership of the Government and the Party, with the wholehearted assistance of the National Assembly and the Front, the successful completion of land reform will help us take a big stride and bring the Resistance war and national construction to victory.

CONGRATULATORY LETTER ON THE VICTORY
AT DIEN BIEN PHU

(addressed to Armymen, War Service Workers, Shock Youth and People in the North-West Area, May 8, 1954.)

Our army has liberated Dien Bien Phu. The Government and I convey our cordial greetings to you, cadres, fighters, war service workers, shock youth and local people who have gloriously fulfilled your tasks.

This victory is big, but it is only the beginning. We must not be self-complacent and subjective and underestimate the enemy. We are determined to fight for independence, national unity, democracy and peace. A struggle, whether military or diplomatic, must be long and hard before complete victory can be achieved.

The Government and I will reward the officers, soldiers, patriotic workers, shock youth and local people who have performed brilliant deeds.

THE NEW SITUATION

(Report to the Sixth Conference of the Central Committee
of the Vietnam Workers' Party — July 15, 1954)

1. The World Situation.

Since the Soviet Union, China and the popular People's
Democracies are in a process of constant development, consolidation and progress in every domain, the world movement for peace and democracy is growing ever stronger.
As a consequence of the wise and correct external policy
of the Soviet Union, the imperialists — and in particular
the American imperialists — have been forced to take part
in the Berlin and Geneva conferences. The mere fact of
these two conferences taking place is already a great victory
for our side, and a defeat for the imperialists.

In the imperialist camp, with the United States in the
lead, contradictions are growing stronger day by day. Here
are some examples.

Contradictions between the English and Americans: They
show themselves in the conflict of interests which divides
Great Britain and the U.S.A. in the Mediterranean, and the
Near and Far East. The Americans are wooing Pakistan,
New Zealand, and Australia, which used to belong to English
sphere of influence. In the Far East there is a clash between
the American and British policies vis-à-vis China and
Japan . . . etc.

Now the contradictions between the French and the
Americans: the Americans are apparently giving the French
all possible help, but in reality this aid is an excuse for
blackmail.

The United States is doing its utmost to force France to sign the Franco-German Treaty, and the treaty concerning the organisation of a European army. France's agreement to this would amount to suicide. As for Indochina, the French and the Americans appear to be in agreement on the war in Vietnam. In reality the Americans, who want to gain control of the puppet regime to oust the French, have given the puppet power to Ngo Dinh Diem, their faithful servant.

The American policy vis-à-vis the "Military Treaty for European Defence" has sown discord both between the countries of West Europe, and inside these countries. The mass of the people are opposed to pro-American governments, and contradictions divide the pro-American capitalists from those who are not pro-American.

In Asia, the Americans propose setting up the SEATO pact with a view to getting Asians to fight Asians. Their policies are extremely reactionary, but they suffer numerous set-backs. They pursue a "policy of force", brandishing the threat of atomic and hydrogen bombs, but the peace movement, opposed to their policies and the use of nuclear weapons, grows stronger day by day. Even the Pope is forced to condemn their policies of using these instruments of mass destruction.

The peace movement has therefore won the great majority of the people, plus a large number of the bourgeoisie of different countries, and even the head of the Roman Catholic Church.

Before the Geneva Conference and before the victory of Dien Bien Phu, the United States intended setting up a "common declaration" between themselves, France, Britain and certain other countries, in which they would threaten China, by accusing her of intervening in the Indo-Chinese war. But the Yankees failed miserably, since Great Britain rejected the proposition, and the other countries had not given their agreement.

Next the Americans preached "common action" with a view to bringing help to the French at Dien Bien Phu.

This led to another failure — their plan received neither the approval of England nor of the other countries. The Americans are doing all they can to sabotage the Geneva Conference — that is to say, to undermine world peace. The U.S. Secretary of State decamped after taking part for a few days only at the Conference; but none the less, the delegations of the other countries continued to sit, and the Conference produced results.

In spite of their failures, the American imperialists have still not learnt their lesson, and persist in their perfidious manoeuvres. They are now busy pushing the formation of the SEATO pact.

Their failures, however, are so many victories for our side. They are the chief enemy of world peace, and we must concentrate our strength against them.

2. The Situation in our Country.

Vietnam, Cambodia and Laos are united, and their resistance grows daily greater. Our guerilla forces in the South, the Centre and the North, are not only staunch and strong but every day put up a stronger resistance.

From the frontier country to Hoa Bin, and the country of the North west etc., our regular army is winning victory after victory.

These victories, including that of Dien Bien Phu, have produced a considerable change in the situation of the country. We have defeated the Navarre plan, and hence produced the fall of the Laniel-Bidault cabinet, and forced the French expeditionary corps to reduce its occupied zones,

Our victories are due to the just policies of our Party and our Government, to the heroism of our army and our people, and to the support of the people of friendly countries, and of people all over the world. They are also the victories of the world movement for peace and democracy.

As well as our success in the military field, we have begun to win battles against feudalism. If our military victories have a good effect on the mobilisation of the masses for the realisation of agrarian reform, our other victories (i.e., against feudalism) have a vital influence on the anti-imperialist struggle.

Our successes fire our people and the peoples of the world, consolidate our diplomatic position at Geneva, and force our enemies to the conference table with us.

The attitude of the French has radically changed in comparison to the conditions put forward by Bollaert in 1947. Thus, since the beginning of the resistance, our position has become stronger and stronger while that of the enemy grows daily weaker. But we must never forget that this strength and this weakness are relative and not absolute. We must not fall into a subjectivist position and underestimate the enemy. Our victories have awoken the Americans. After the battle of Dien Bien Phu, they changed their plans for intervention to prolong the Indo Chinese war, to internationalise it, to sabotage the Geneva Conference and to seek for all means to oust the French and gain control of Vietnam, Cambodia and Laos and make these three peoples into their slaves and increase international tension. The Americans are not only the enemies of the people of the whole world — they are becoming the principal and direct enemies of the peoples of Vietnam, Cambodia and Laos.

The Conference of Geneva met following the changes arising, as I have shown above, in the national and international situation. At the conference, one can see the deepening of the already existing contradictions between the imperialists: the French would like to negotiate, the English take no clear position, the Americans sabotage it. At the present moment the latter are becoming more and more isolated.

Vietnam, China and the Soviet Union are more united than ever before. As a result of the contradictions between the imperialists, and thanks to our efforts and those of our camp, we have arrived at some fairly important agreements. The French government is now in the hands of those who favour peace, and chances are offered us to arrive at a cessation of hostilities in Indo-China.

During the provisional suspension of the Geneva Conference, the heads of the delegations have returned to their country after having conferred their powers to their assistants.

Profiting from this occasion, Comrade Chou En-lai, Prime Minister of the People's Republic of China, paid a visit to India and Burma. With the Prime Ministers of these countries, he signed two common declarations on peace. The five principles set forth in the declarations are brief, but completely clear and just, and have been greatly welcomed by the peoples of the whole world, particularly those in Asia; at the same time they have put a check to American manoeuvres to sow discord among the peoples of Asia.

Here is the content of their agreements:

1. Mutual respect for sovereignty and territorial integrity.
2. Non-aggression.
3. Non-interference in the internal affairs of each country.
4. Relations of friendship and equality.
5. Peaceful co-existence.

My interview with Comrade Chou also gave good results. His friendly meetings with the representatives of India, Burma and Vietnam, have brought a closer unity to the peoples of Asia. That is yet another success to the credit of our camp.

The situation in the world, in our country and in Asia, means that we can win peace. But the U.S.A. continue with their sabotage, the advocates of war still exist in France, and the pro-American puppets redouble their efforts at sabotage. That is why the continuation of war still remains possible. That is the characteristic of the new situation of our country.

3. Our new tasks

The new situation poses new problems; implies new directives and new tactics. In the course of these nine years of resistance, after a heroic struggle under the leadership of the Party and the Government, and at the cost of countless difficulties, our army and our people have won staggering victories. Our forces have made progress in every sense. The successes we have won are due to the just policies of the Party and the Government. At the present moment, the situation having taken a new turn, our tasks are not exactly the same and our policies and our slogans have consequently had to be equally modified. Up to now we have concentrated our strength to destroy that of the imperialist French aggressors. At the present moment, the French are negotiating with us, while the American imperialists are now becoming our principle direct enemies.

Our principle struggle must be waged against the latter. From now to the re-establishment of peace, we will continue to fight the French. But it is against the Americans that our struggle and that of the peoples of the entire world must converge. The policy of the United States is to extend and internationalise the Indo-Chinese war — our aim, to fight for peace against the war policy of the Americans. For nine years the programme of our Party has emphasised the following objectives:

Vietnam, Cambodia and Laos must be completely independent and freed from the French yoke; rejection of the French Union: expulsion of the French expeditionary force from Indo-China; destruction of the puppet regime and army, confiscation of the property of the imperialists and of all the collaborators; agitation for the reduction of farm rents and work for land reform; achievement of democracy over the whole country, and resistance until final victory.

This programme has obtained many successes and has been proved just.

But, faced with the new situation, it cannot remain just as it stands. In the new contingencies the old slogan of "Resistance to the end" must be replaced with "Peace, national unity, independence, democracy". Against the U.S.

aims of intervention, of prolongation and extension of the Indo-Chinese war, we must hold the flag of peace aloft, and our policies must in consequence be modified. Before, we talked of the confiscation of the property of the French imperialists; but now that they are negotiating with us, they could, following the principle of equality and reciprocal advantages, maintain their economic and cultural interests in Indo-China.

When two sides negotiate, they make reasonable reciprocal concessions.

In the past we used to say "search ont and destroy the French expeditionary corps to the last man". At present, in the negotiations, we have put forward, and the French have accepted, the withdrawal of the armies at a given date.

Before, the French Union did not exist for us. Now we have agreed to consider the question of our possible participation in the French Union, on the principle of equality and free agreement. Before, we proposed the complete destruction of the puppet army and regime with a view to national unity; now we are putting forward a generous measure, national reunification by means of general elections over the whole of the country.

To re-establish peace you have to stop hostilities, which is done by a cease-fire. But before arriving at this, it is necessary to demarcate the zones. The enemy army has to be regrouped in a given zone with a view to its progressive withdrawal, and our army has to assemble in another zone.

We need a vast region uniting all the necessary conditions for the building up of our forces and for their consolidation and development. It must be a region whose influence on the other regions will lead to national reunification. Demarcating the zones for the regroupment of the armies does not mean that we are dividing the country — it is a provisional measure to produce national reunification.

When the demarcation and exchange of regroupment zones has been effected, our compatriots inhabiting regions up till now free, but which will provisionally be occupied by the enemy, will indeed have food for discontent — some will see only the black side; they will despair and may let themselves be used by our enemies.

We must make them clearly understand that in the interests of the whole country in the long-term interest, one must learn to endure the present. To do this will be to their honour — the nation will be grateful to them. We must try to banish negative pessimism from everybody. Everyone must continue to exert all their strength in demanding that the French withdraw their troops so that independence can be achieved.

Our aim and principle, therefore, is the delimitation of zones to lead to peace and to use general elections in the whole country to obtain national unity. We lead the resistance for independence, unity, democracy and peace. The re-establishment of peace will also lead to independence, unity and democracy. The new situation necessitates a new political line with a view to new successes.

Whether we have to work in peace or continue the war we must retain the initiative, and foresee and prepare the future.

It is not an easy thing to win the peace. It is a long, hard and complex struggle, with its difficulties and its favourable factors. The friendly countries and the peoples of the world support us; our people are full of ardour and confidence in our Party and our Government; under a wise leadership the people will unite for the peacetime struggle, just as they did in the war of resistance — these are the favourable factors. And here are our difficulties: the Americans do all they can to sabotage peace in Indo-China, and the peace supporters in France still remain under Yankee influence.

The new situation is not only proving to be difficult, it still remains complex. Thus we have to have a different line for the newly liberated regions and the old liberated regions, for our free zone and for the zone that is provisionally reserved for the regroupment of the enemy forces. Before, we only had rural problems, now we need a policy for the towns. As for the French, our policy towards them will also be different from the one we followed in the past. Equally, we must treat pro-American and pro-French traitors differently. In the past we only had our own internal policy and diplomatic relations with friendly countries; now our diplomatic relations extend yet further to other countries.

We must make a distinction between immediate and long-term interests, between local and general interests.

This situation, complex and full of difficulties, is in full evolution. It follows that changes will take place in the outlook of the people and the cadres. If they lack the necessary preparation and correct leadership, disorder in thought and action will follow. The following errors could take place: leftist deviation — people drunk with our continued victories will want to go on fighting at whatever cost, and fight to the end. Like a man who sees only the tree, not the forest, they will see the retreat of the enemy without seeing his manoeuvres; they will see the French without seeing the Americans; they will be all for military action, and will underestimate diplomatic action. They will not understand that, parallel to the armed struggle, we carry on our fight in the international conferences with the same objective in view. They are opposed to new slogans, which they consider as so many right-wing manifestations and ill-considered concessions; they put forward excessive conditions, unacceptable to the enemy. They want to precipitate everything and do not realise that the struggle for peace is hard and complex. If we yield to leftism, we will be isolated, cut off from our people and from the peoples of the world, and we will suffer a setback.

Right-wing deviation manifests itself in a negative pessimism and concessions without principle. Having no faith in the strength of the people, the right-wingers weaken the people's will to struggle. They forget the habit of suffering, the ability to endure and only aspire to a quiet and easy life.

Leftism as well as right-wing deviation are both errors. They will be equally exploited by the enemy and will be profitable to him and harmful to us.

4. *Concrete tasks and work*

The new situation poses three new tasks:

1) To win and consolidate the peace, and to obtain national unity as well as independence and democracy in the whole of the country.

2) To develop the armed force of the people, to create a powerful peoples' army, competent to withstand the exigencies of the new situation.

3) Continue to carry out the slogan "The land to those who work it", to work for a rise in production, and to prepare the conditions for national reconstruction.

These three aims need ten different tasks:

1) Realise a unity of view throughout the Party and among the whole people as regards the situation and the new tasks.

2) Improve the leadership of the diplomatic struggle.

3) Do all we can to increase the strength of the peoples' army.

4) Take responsibility for the newly liberated regions; particularly take responsibility for the management of the towns.

5) Change the orientation of labour in the zone provisionally occupied by enemy troops.

6) Continue to consolidate the old free zone.

7) Pursue vigorously the mobilisation of the masses to carry out agrarian reform.

8) Improve economic and financial work and prepare the conditions for national construction.

9) Help the national liberation movement of the Laotian and Cambodian peoples.

10) Continue to rectify the work of the Party, reorganise the Party in the newly liberated regions.

These ten tasks will all be carried out under the leadership of the Central Committee. Each locality and branch will not have to undertake all ten of these works but only a certain number of them.

Of all of these tasks, ideological leadership is the most important. An exact understanding of the situation and the new tasks is the precondition both in and out of the Party for the unity of thought necessary for any unity of action. Our tasks and our work, however, heavy, difficult and complex they may be, will certainly be crowned with success if the unity of thought and unity of action can be realised from top to bottom, both inside and outside of the Party.

At this moment American imperialism, the principal enemy of the peoples of the world, is becoming the direct principal enemy of the peoples of Indo-China; that is why all our actions must be aimed at this one enemy.

Any person and any country which is not pro-American will be able, even if only temporarily, to form a united front with us.

Our unchangeable objectives remain — peace, independence, unity, democracy. Our principles must be firm, but our tactics flexible. The various tasks must be co-ordinated and linked one to another, and the Party must give its support to all these tasks.

Every job must correspond exactly to a given locality, moment and situation.

With the correct leadership of the Party and the Government, the unity and effort of all the cadres and the whole people, with the approval and support of the friendly countries and all peace-loving peoples in the world, we will certainly succeed in the fulfilment of the three aims and the ten tasks I have just outlined.

APPEAL MADE AFTER THE SUCCESSFUL CONCLUSION
OF THE GENEVA AGREEMENTS

(July 22, 1954)

Compatriots all over the country,
Armymen and cadres,
The Geneva Conference has come to an end. It is a great victory for our diplomacy.

On behalf of the Government, I cordially make the following appeal:

(1) For the sake of peace, unity, independence and democracy of the Fatherland, our people, armymen, cadres and government have, during these eight years or so, joined in a monolithic bloc, endured hardship and overcome all difficulties to resolutely carry out the Resistance and have won many brilliant victories. On this occasion, on behalf of the Government, I cordially congratulate you, from North to South. I respectfully bow to the memory of the armymen and people who have sacrificed their lives for the Fatherland, and send my homage and sympathy to the wounded and sick armymen.

This great victory is also due to the support given us in our just struggle by the peoples of our brother countries, by the French people and the peace-loving people of the world.

Thanks to these victories and the efforts made by the delegation of the Soviet Union at the Berlin Conference, negotiations were opened between our country and France at the Geneva Conference. At this conference the struggle of our delegation and the assistance given by the delegations of the Soviet Union and China have ended in a great victory for us; the French government has recognised the independence, sovereignty, unity and territorial integrity of our country; it has agreed to withdraw French troops from our country, etc.

From now on, we must make every effort to consolidate peace and achieve reunification, independence and democracy throughout our country.

(2) In order to re-establish peace, the first step to take is that the armed forces of both parties should cease fire.

The regroupment in two regions is a temporary measure; it is a transitional step for the implementation of the armistice and restoration of peace, and paves the way for national reunification through general elections. Regroupment in regions is in no way a partition of our country, neither is it an administrative division.

During the armistice, our army is regrouped in the North; the French troops are regrouped in the South, that is to say, there is a change of regions. A number of regions which were formerly occupied by the French, now become our free zones. Vice versa, a number of regions formerly liberated by us, will now be temporarily occupied by the French troops before they leave for France.

This is a necessity; North, Central and South Viet Nam are territories of ours. Our country will certainly be unified, our entire people will surely be liberated.

Our compatriots in the South were the first to wage the war of Resistance. They possess a high political consciousness. I am confident that they will place national interests above local interests, permanent interests above temporary interests, and join their efforts with the entire people in strengthening peace, achieving unity, independence and democracy all over the country. The Party, Government and I always follow the efforts of our people and we are sure that our compatriots will be victorious.

(3) The struggle to consolidate peace and achieve reunification, independence and democracy, is also a long and hard struggle. In order to carry the day, our people, armymen and cadres, from North to South, must unite closely. They must be at one in thought and deed.

We are resolved to abide by the agreements entered into with the French Government. At the same time we demand that the French Government should correctly implement the agreements they have signed with us.

We must do our utmost to strengthen peace, and be vigilant to check the manoeuvres of peace wreckers.

We must endeavour to struggle for the holding of free general elections throughout the country to reunify our territory.

We must exert all our efforts to restore, build, strengthen and develop our forces in every field so as to attain complete independence.

We must do our utmost to carry out social reforms in order to improve our people's livelihood and realise genuine democracy.

We further tighten our fraternal relations with Cambodia and Laos.

We strengthen the great friendship between us and the Soviet Union, China and other brother countries. To maintain peace, we enhance our solidarity with the French people, the Asian people and people all over the world.

(4) I call on all our compatriots, armymen and cadres to strictly follow the lines and policies laid down by the Party and Government, to struggle for the consolidation of peace, and the achievement of national reunification, independence and democracy throughout the country.

I eagerly appeal to all genuine patriots, irrespective of their social class, creed, political stand and former affiliation, sincerely to co-operate with us and fight for the sake of our country and our people so as to bring about peace and achieve reunification, independence and democracy for our beloved Vietnam.

If our people are as one, if thousands of men are like one, victory will certainly be ours.

Long live a peaceful, unified, independent and democratic Vietnam !

The First Land Reform Drive at Thai Nguyen

(September 12, 1954)

In land rent reduction and land reform, a number of cadres were very good in implementing the policies, but others made mistakes by following roundabout paths, thus causing a great loss of time, while the result obtained was not up to expectations. In land rent reduction and land reform, we must fully grasp the policies and political line, clearly know where our main forces lie, base ourselves on the poor and landless peasants and unite with the middle peasants. That is why the Party and government have always pointed out the necessity for unity of the toiling peasants. If this is done, all work will be successfully carried out, if not, our work will not make headway, there will be a time lag and the result will be poor.

We must know how to discriminate between landlords. They are the peasants' enemies, but they are not united. If discrimination can be made, our work will be easier. When this point was studied, many cadres believed that they understood, but in practice their work turned out to be erroneous. Some of them thought it was better to deviate to the "left" than to the "right". That is not so, for, left or right, either side is far from reality. We must grasp the policies, rely on the masses and differentiate between landlords.

In your work, you have all obtained a number of achievements despite shortcomings. Your success in this drive is that, in applying the "three withs":

> "Eat with the peasants,
> Live with the peasants,
> Work with the peasants",

94

you have been better able to endure hardships. In the fourth rent reduction drive many cadres only applied the principle of "one with" or "two withs" or "two and a half withs", but not the complete "three withs". It must be realised that only by carrying out the "three withs" can one become familiar with the peasants, understand their feelings, mobilise them to overthrow landlordism and successfully carry out land rent reduction and land reform. Without this principle, one stands aloof from the masses, and cannot work efficiently. Therefore in the next drive, you must apply the "three withs" unreservedly. From generation to generation our peasants were doomed to live in poverty. Considering their situation, a few months in which to apply the "three withs" is an insignificant period. But what else can be done?

As far as internal unity is concerned, older cadres must help new cadres. You did it fairly well in this drive. But this does not mean that there were no shortcomings. A number of older cadres were too proud of themselves for having taken part in many drives. They did not take the trouble to study instructions from higher levels and were not willing to help the new cadres. Bear in mind that, as the situation changes constantly, lack of study means regress, and regression means failure.

A rather prevalent mistake is: the desire to rest. There are cadres who, after serving in a few drives, now want to settle in towns. They are wrong. Here is an example; "Who has struggled longer, you or I?" (Everybody answered: You). My struggle was longer and I never asked for a rest, why do you, after a few drives, want to have a rest?

You want to rest and to settle in town, because you have not yet realised the importance of land reform. You have certainly read the Party's resolution, "Land reform is one of the three cardinal tasks laid down by the Party and the government." The desire to settle in town, not to take part in land reform, is *shirking duty*.

Wherever the Party and government send you, you must at any cost fulfil the task entrusted by them, and not follow your own bent.

What do you want? To take part in the Revolution. Well, land reform is a revolutionary task. "Don't believe that the surrounding mountain tops are higher than that on which you are standing".

You must understand that land reform is one of the three primary tasks laid down for the Party, the Government and the people. It is a glorious and heavy task. The fighter is not only the man who kills the enemy at the front. You are fighters, too; fighters on the antifeudal front. As fighters, you cannot say that you want to go to this front and not to that front, you must fulfil your duty as fighters. When the land reform is carried through, you will have a rest. As long as it is not achieved, you cannot enjoy one.

You must firmly grasp the Party's and government's policies, overcome difficulties, and labour under hardship to discharge your duty.

During the Resistance war, our army won victory upon victory. As a fighter on the anti-feudal front, you must be resolved to win.

Heroes are not only to be found among the soldiers at the battlefront. They can be found among you, fighting on the antifeudal front together with the peasants. In this conference there are people who during the last land-rent reduction and land reform drives, have done good work in linking up their main tasks with mobilising the peasants to increase production, to combat drought and flood, and to engage in voluntary labour or to join the army. With the responsible committee, you will select the best men and women among you; the Party, government and I will reward them.

In the coming mass mobilisation drives for land-rent reduction and land reform, those among you who perform outstanding deeds, will be awarded medals, just like soldiers fighting the enemy. It is up to you to decide upon this reward. Those who wish to receive medals must do their best.

(Extract from speech delivered May 6, 1955)

Most of you came from communes where land reform has been realised. You found that rent reduction and land reform at the beginning were not easy. Now, the organisation of mutual aid teams is also not easy. Those who think it easy will fall into subjectivism and meet failure.

The organisation of mutual aid teams should be carried out according to correct principles and method.

The present policy is to develop a great number of work exchange teams, per season or per specific work, so that such teams can be found in all the places where rent reduction and land reform have been carried out. Wherever the people's and cadres' political standards are high, we shall organise exchange of labour, in permanence or from one season's cultivation to another. Wherever such exchange of labour already exists, we have to consolidate it and make it better.

Firstly, compulsion should not be used with anybody. By means of propaganda, we should explain to the peasants the advantages of the mutual aid teams; we should give them complete freedom of adherence, and strictly refrain from any compulsion.

Secondly, the families should find interests after joining the mutual aid teams. The peasants will confidently join the teams only when they find it is in their interest. To convince people to join such teams is not an easy job. But even when this has been done, we are not yet successful because the peasantry is fraught with many complicated questions. For instance, in each team there are big families and small ones, people who can work hard and others who cannot,

97

families which have buffaloes and others which have not. Even among draught animals, some are strong, others are weak. Some lands are nearby, others are far away. When the crop simultaneously gets ripe on many fields, everybody wants to have his own harvested first. If these questions are not settled in the interests of everybody, they will give rise to dissatisfaction and jealousy among the people. It is failure then.

Thirdly, a mutual aid team should be headed by a team leader or a managing committee. The management should be democratic. Every task should be discussed among the team members. When they have understood the utility of the task, they will be willing to do it. If we force people to do work of which they do not understand the utility, the work will meet with failure.

Address to the Closing Session of the Vietnam Fatherland Front Congress

(September, 1955)

After several days of hard work and animated discussion, the Congress has unanimously adopted the new Manifesto of the Fatherland Front. This is another victory.

We can say that this is a Manifesto of Broad Unity, the aim of which is to struggle for peace, reunification, independence and democracy for the whole country.

Everybody must recognise that the Manifesto of the Front is very firm, broad and practical.

It is practical because it is in perfect agreement with the deep aspirations of our countrymen from North to South. Apart from a handful of individuals who have sold out their conscience to the U.S. imperialists, all Vietnamese wish that their country should be reunified, and reunified through peaceful means. Therefore, if all members of the Front endeavour to make the people understand the significance of the Manifesto, the great majority will certainly welcome and support the Manifesto.

The Manifesto is a broad one because it reads: the Front is ready to welcome into its ranks all those who are sincerely opposed to the U.S.-Diem schemes to divide the country, and sincerely support national unity. The Front is ready to unite with all patriots whatever their political tendencies or their religions. Thus the Front will include persons who now sincerely want to serve the Fatherland, whatever parties or groups they may have belonged to in the past.

It is a firm one because the Front is based on the great majority of the people made up of workers and peasants, and at the same time covers all strata in our society.

The Fatherland Front is supported by the great majority of our people. It will be supported by all peaceloving people throughout the world.

This practical, broad and firm character will ensure a glorious future for the Front.

I avail myself of this occasion to express a few opinions:

— The Front has produced a correct Manifesto. This is very good for the coming struggle. But this is only the first step on the road leading to complete victory. From now on, we have to struggle hard to put the Manifesto into practice. This struggle will be fraught with difficulties and hardships. We must show patience and determination. The first and most urgent thing we have to do is to make everyone acquainted with the Manifesto, and make it clearly understood and widely known from North to South, so that everyone may fully grasp the spirit and contents of the Manifesto and wholeheartedly support it.

— The North is the foundation the root of our people's struggle. Only when the foundation is firm, does the house stand firm. Only when the root is strong, will the tree grow well. To put the Front's Manifesto into practice, we must endeavour to consolidate the North in every way, we must make the North progress steadily and become strong; we should certainly not allow the consolidation of the North to slow down.

To make the North progress and become strong, is to take practical account of the South.

Some people have said: The Front has produced a good Manifesto. But in case the U.S.-Diem clique do not budge, what shall we do?

Here is the answer: By its very nature, a stone will not budge of itself. But when many people join hands, a bloc of stone, however heavy it may be, can be moved.

We are united and resolved to consolidate the North, to put into practice the Front's Manifesto; thus we shall have a very great thrusting force. And the U.S.-Diem clique, although they want to stay, will not be able to do so, and although they do not want to move, they will have to.

100

That is why we should not ask: "What if the U.S.-Diem clique do not budge?" But each of us should ask himself: "What efforts have I made? Have I done my duty?" If all of us endeavour to consolidate the North and to put into practice the Front's Manifesto, we will, with the support of peace-loving people in the world, force them to move.

MASS EDUCATION

(Address to a Conference reviewing the progress of mass education in the first half of 1956, July 16, 1956)

On behalf of the Party and Government, I inquire after your health — cadres and mass education fighters — and congratulate the mass education service on its achievements during the first six months of the year. Over the past six months, 2,100,000 persons attended classes. This is a great achievement. Formerly, in the imperialist and feudal days, over 90 per cent of our population were illiterate. Later, the late Mr. Nguyen Van To and a number of progressive people worked for the popularisation of the national script. They made great efforts but only 5,000 persons per year went to classes. In the first six months of this year, there were over two million pupils. This is a great achievement, but we should not consider it as sufficient, we should make further efforts and avoid self-conceit and complacency.

After seven days of discussion and exchange of experiences, you are now probably more experienced than I am. But I would like to contribute a number of my own experiences.

(1) In order to wipe out illiteracy among the great masses, where the overwhelming majority are peasants, the education movement should be a mass movement. We should stand close to the masses, discuss with them, apply forms and methods suitable to their life, and rely upon them to promote the movement.

Formerly, a number of other cadres and I carried out clandestine revolutionary activities in Cao Bang. The majority of our compatriots there were Nung, Man, and Tho, who knew little Vietnamese, lived scattered in the mountains far from one another, and were busy with their work and both teaching and studying had to be done in secret. We carried out mass education in these difficult conditions, but we succeeded. The cadres drafted a plan, in consultation with our compatriots, and the latter told them what to do. The literate taught the illiterate, those who knew much taught those who knew little.

Classes were run in caves; each village sent a person to study for a few days, then he went back and taught his co-villagers. When his knowledge was exhausted he returned to the class and learned some more. While teaching others, the teachers also learned themselves. Such was the method we adopted for the mass education work and for its development into a movement.

At that time, in spite of the enemy restrictions and continuous persecutions, our compatriots were very studious, women and children being more studious than men. At present, on my visits to the classes, I also find that women and children are more numerous than men. Many men have not attended classes yet. There were no classes or schools then; people who went weeding or gathering vegetables appointed a place and went there to teach one another. Cadres going to the fields to work were often stopped by the villagers and asked to hear them recite lessons; if the lessons were wrongly read out, the cadres would correct them; if they had been well learned, the cadres would be asked to give a new lesson.

Workers and peasants have a lot of work to do. If the method of teaching is not suitable to the learners, to their work and mode of life, if we expect classes provided with tables and benches, we cannot be successful. The organisation of teaching should be in accordance with the living conditions of the learners, then the movement will last and bear good results. Our compatriots are still poor and cannot afford paper and pens, therefore a small pocket exercise-book is enough for each person. Reading and writing exercises can be done anywhere, using charcoal, the ground or banana leaves as pens and paper. Clandestine cadres were to teach and make one person literate every three months. At that time, there was no assistance from the Government, no Ministry, or department in charge of educational problems but in such precarious conditions, the movement kept developing, like oil spreading, the literate teaching the illiterate.

In studying as in teaching, the youth is the main force of the mass education movement. Everywhere, we should make the youth understand this task. In teaching as well as in studying the youth must always be in the van.

(2) Mass education work is also teaching work, but not in schools or classes provided with lamps and books as in general schools. It is a wide, complicated, and self-sufficient movement. General schools are divided into first, second third, and fourth forms, but in mass education, there are students of all kinds, the young, the old, some know much others just a little, some assimilate quickly, others slowly therefore this is a hard task which requires much patience and effort. The fear of difficulties and hardships is not admissible in mass education. Sometimes, we have to come and teach a mother of many children at her own house. With those aged people who are reluctant to attend classes, we should patiently convince them to do so or sometimes come and teach them in their own houses. In order to wipe out illiteracy from among the people, industriousness is indispensable, bureaucracy and ordering about are impossible

The work is inconvenient and hard, and gives no fame at all. In the Resistance war, if we succeeded in killing many of the enemy we could become model fighters or heroes; working in factories, if we make many innovations or surpass the production target, we become also outstanding workers or labour heroes. Mass education work, though not giving us fame, nor being a well-sounding job, is however very glorious. We should not stand in one place and wish for another one; we should not nourish the wrong intention of giving up mass education work and entering a technical school or teaching in a general school or taking another profession

In social life there are many professions, a division of work is therefore inevitable. I do one job, you take up another. Mass education work is an important one, having a great bearing on the nation and society, and also on the building of our Fatherland. Although not a well-sounding, famous or outstanding job which makes one become a hero, it is really a very important one. A person who is now a mass education worker should refrain from the desire of assuming another profession.

(3) Mass education work is also placed under leadership. We have the Ministry, the Department, the Zonal and the Provincial services. To lead is not to sit and write office notes at the desk. In the Resistance time, there were cadres who could draft a good programme for secondary education but were unable to take charge of a mass education class because they were always in the office. The leaders should closely unite with and assist the cadres to overcome difficulties; bureaucracy and ordering about are to be avoided. In any work, close connection with the people is essential, mass education services at all levels should correct their own mistakes if any, and learn from the experience of others.

(4) Formerly, being poor, workers and peasants could not send their children to school; only a small number of children could attend class, the majority of these were from well-to-do families which had enough food to eat. In the countryside, only the children of landlords and rich peasants could go to school. Some cadres put the question as to whether the children of landlords and rich peasants should be allowed to teach in a mass education class. This is posing the question incorrectly. Any youth, male or female, is given this job if he or she is good, otherwise the work will not be entrusted to them. A worthy young person who does not approve his or her parents' exploitations and does not side with them to act against the people, will be accepted as a teacher in a mass education class. If he or she has committeed serious faults, the job will not be given to them, either in mass education work or any other work. If a certain young person, whose parents are guilty landlords, does not follow his or her parents, he or she is not guilty and can maintain citizenship rights like other young people. He or she can

attend classes or take part in public work or join people's organisations. This point should be well understood and correctly applied by you who live in the countryside.

(5) Mass education work, though apparently not heroic, can be of a very great service to the nation if it can wipe out illiteracy among the people in three years. Our country would be proud of having rapidly eliminated illiteracy. In so-called civilised countries such as the U.S.A., Great Britain and France, there are still some illiterate people. To wipe out illiteracy in two or three years is a very great victory. We should realise this and make further efforts. By so doing, it will not be this young man or that young woman who becomes a hero, but all cadres and teachers working for mass education will be heroes; and collective heroes are all the better.

If illiteracy is wiped out in three years, new tasks are set for the Government, the Ministry of Education, and the Ministry of Culture; you too, you will be faced with new tasks. It does not mean when everybody knows how to read and write, you will have fulfilled your tasks and you may rest or take up other work.

Illiterate people should learn to become literate. When they have learned to read, they should push further in their studies. Literate people will fall into illiteracy again if they have no reading materials. The Government and the Ministry of Education have therefore the task of furnishing books and newspapers suited to the standards of these readers.

You have the task of helping our illiterate compatriots to become literate, then to push forward their studies. So you yourselves should push forward your studies in order to be able to teach at a higher level. Our nation goes forward, the cadres should also go forward. They should march in the lead in order to ensure the continuous progress of the nation.

A TALK WITH INTELLECTUALS

(Extract from address to students at the Political Course of the Vietnam People's University, July 21, 1956)

I am very pleased to see that despite the difference of ages, professions, and abilities, you are all prompted by the same will, that is to make progress so as to serve the Fatherland and the people more effectively. That single-mindedness has resulted in your solidarity even in this class. Unity is the force which leads us to all victories.

Here are some ideas of mine for your consideration.

Revolutionary forces: The main revolutionary forces are the workers and peasants. The reason for this is that they are the producers of all wealth that keep Society alive, and that they make up the most numerous and also the most heavily exploited section of the population. It is also because their revolutionary spirit is firmer and more persevering than that of all other social strata.

However, the revolution also needs the force of intellectuals (generally called brain workers). For instance; doctors are necessary for the preservation of people's health; teachers for the education of people and the training of cadres; engineers for economic construction, etc.

So, brain workers play an important and glorious role in the revolution and in socialist construction; *and workers, peasants, and intellectuals should be closely united as one bloc.*

Close link with the workers and peasants: The colonialist and feudal regimes have deliberately separated the intellectuals from the bloc of workers and peasants. They have created the thought that "Everything but book-learning is worthless". They used intellectuals in their ruling apparatus for their own profits. To sow dissension between brain workers and manual workers is also part of their "divide and rule" policy.

Nowadays, such severance should be gradually wiped out, and the working people (brain workers and manual workers) should be closely united in order to join efforts in the building of a new and happy society.

I am of the opinion that, on the way towards unity, intellectuals should take the initiative in making the first step to come to the workers and peasants; I am sure they will be warmly welcomed by the latter.

Method of study: To study is a lifelong matter. Theory should be closely coupled with practical work. No one can pretend to have sufficient or thorough knowledge. The world changes every day. Our people are progressing day by day. We should therefore continue to study and practise what we have learnt so as to keep pace with the people's progress.

The time you spend in class being relatively short, *the object of your studies cannot be too great nor too high.* What you learn here can be compared to a small seed. Later, you must continue to take care of that seed. You must make it grow into a plant, then make the plant gradually blossom and bear fruit.

In my personal opinion, that seed can be described in these eleven words "Dai hoc chi dao, tai minh minh duc, tai than dan" (The doctrine of University education consists in promoting lofty virtues and in uniting with the people).

Briefly speaking, "minh minh duc" means *to have righteous mind,* and "than dan", *to serve the people* and put the people's interests above all.

In other words, "to undergo sufferings before the people, and to enjoy happiness after the people".

We all have more or less inherited the thoughts, habits and manners of the old society. Therefore, it is not easy to materialise the two words "chinh tam" (righteous mind).

We have to go through a struggle between the old and the new in ourselves, an arduous, hard and unremitting struggle but if we are resolute, the new will win over the old and the righteousness of mind will achieve success.

Freedom of thought: Our regime being a democratic one, there should be freedom of thought. What is freedom? In all matters, everyone is free to express his own view, thereby contributing to the establishing of the truth. That is a right and also a duty of all people.

After everyone's view has been expressed and truth has been established, freedom of thought turns into *freedom to obey the truth.*

Truth is what is beneficial to the Fatherland and to the people. What is detrimental to the interests of the Fatherland and people is not truth. To strive to serve the Fatherland and the people is to obey the truth.

Attitude of the Party and the Government towards intellectuals: As a part of the revolutionary forces, intellectuals have the task of carrying out emulation for serving the Fatherland and the people. Our Party and Government therefore *highly appreciate the people's intellectuals who work for the people.*

To build the country, an increasing number of good intellectuals is required. The Party and Government should on the one hand help the present generation of intellectuals to progress day by day and on the other hand strive to train new intellectuals.

The Party and Government should help the intellectuals by educating them so as to give them a firm class stand, a correct viewpoint, sound thinking, and democratic manners. In short, intellectuals should be helped to achieve a righteous mind and close connections with the people.

As far as the method of education is concerned, it should follow the principle of voluntariness and self-consciousness. There should be explanations, discussions, and persuasion instead of compulsion. Intellectuals should be helped to emulate each other in their studies and work. They should also be shown how to practise the method of "sincere self-criticism and frank criticism" so that all of them may make uninterrupted progress, unite with one another, and serve the Fatherland and people.

SPEECH INAUGURATING THE FIRST THEORETICAL COURSE
OF NGUYEN AI QUOC SCHOOL

(September 7, 1957)

I have dealt with the importance of theoretical study and now I shall speak of integration of theory with practice. Theory is very necessary but unmethodical study yields no result. Therefore in studying theory we have to stress that: *theory must be integrated with practice.*

Unity of theory and practice is a fundamental principle of Marxism-Leninism. Practice without the guidance of theory is blind practice. Theory without integration with practice is mere theory. For that reason while laying stress on the importance of theory, Lenin repeated over and over again that revolutionary theory is not dogma but a guide to revolutionary action; and that it is not something rigid, but of a rich creative nature; that theory needs be constantly improved by new conclusions drawn from living practice. Communists of various countries must put Marxism-Leninism in concrete form proper to circumstances of the given time and of the given place.

The Party school is the school to train outstanding fighters devoted to the proletarian cause. You are all high-ranking cadres of the Party. Your theoretical study does not aim at turning you into mere theoreticians, but at enabling you to work well. It means that you must study the spirit of Marxism-Leninism, its stand, viewpoint and method, to put them into practice in order satisfactorily to solve practical problems in our revolutionary work. How is theory integrated with practice?

— We study theory in order to apply it, not for its own sake, and not to make a capital for ourselves later to bargain with the Party. All bad motives should be extirpated.

— We do not carry on studies to learn by heart every sentence and every word and apply the experience of brother countries in a mechanical way. We must learn Marxism-Leninism to analyse and solve the actual issues of the revolution in our country according to its particular conditions.

Reality is problems to be solved, and contradictions lying within things. We are revolutionary cadres, our reality is problems to be solved that the revolution puts to us. Real life is immense. It covers the experience drawn from the work and thought of an individual, the Party's policies and line, its historical experiences and issues at home and in the world. In the course of our study these are realities to be kept in contact with.

However, in this school we must primarily compare theory with our thought and work, that is to use the theory we have acquired to make an analysis of the success and failure in our work, and discover the origin of our correct or wrong stand, viewpoint and method. To do so is to sum up in order to improve our approach to these issues and to work with better results. We carry out the revolution with a view to transforming the world and society.

In our study, we have also to bring into focus the actual issues in the country and in the world, the revolutionary problems and tasks ahead of our Party, using the acquired understanding to find the correct line and method for the solving of these issues, or to analyse the experiences drawn from work done by the Party and to discover the causes of its successes and failures. This will help us consolidate our stand and enhance our viewpoint and method.

However, it is necessary to refrain from demanding the solving of all actual issues in the course of the study. The practice of the revolution is very extensive and the solving of all the issues put forth by this practice is a long-term work for the whole Party. At school we can only lay the foundation for integration of theory with practice. The experience of brother Parties as well as ours has given many lessons in the harm done by *dogmatism* divorced from real life.

Thanks to its ability in combining Marxism — Leninism with the actual situation of our country, our Party has scored many successes in its work. However, the combination of Marxist — Leninist truth with the practice of the Vietnamese revolution was not complete and brought about many mistakes, namely those committed in the land reform, readjustment of organisation and economic construction. At present, in building socialism, although we have the rich experiences of brother countries, we cannot apply them mechanically because our country has its own peculiarities. Disregard for the peculiarities of one's nation while learning from the experiences of the brother countries is a serious mistake, is dogmatism. But undue emphasis on the role of national peculiarities and negation of the universal value of the great, basic experiences of the brother countries will lead to grave revisionist mistakes.

For that reason, while laying emphasis on the importance of theoretical study, stress must always be laid on the principle of integrating theory with practice. We have to overcome dogmatism, and to be also on our guard against *revisionism*. In short, we must be aware of the importance of theory to study enthusiastically. In the course of your study, only by making use of what you will have learned to analyse and solve the practical questions in your ideological work and in the Party, can you obtain good results.

THE OCTOBER REVOLUTION AND THE LIBERATION OF THE PEOPLES OF THE EAST

(extracts from an article written for the National Political Publishing House of the U.S.S.R on the 40th Anniversary of the October Revolution, 1957)

Like the rising sun driving away the shadows, the October Revolution brightened the history of mankind with a new dawn.

Forty years ago under the leadership of the Leninist Party, the Russian proletariat, firmly united with the working peasants, overthrew the power of the capitalists and landlords. The Soviet state, the state of proletarian dictatorship, bringing a genuine democracy to the people, has given proof of its vitality and invincible strength.

The October Revolution was the victory of the revolutionary forces of the toiling masses; it was an extremely violent upheaval creating conditions which clearly showed the creativeness of the toiling masses. The victory of the October Revolution confirmed the correctness of Marxism-Leninism; it paved the way to new victories of the working class in social life, on the basis of great loyalty to Marxist-Leninist principles. Thanks to the clear-sightedness and heroism of the Leninist Party, the Party of the proletarian class, the October Revolution won victory and ushered in a new era in the history of mankind and a new stage on the long and glorious path covered by the revolutionary Party of the Russian proletariat.

Owing to the success of the October Revolution, the Leninist Party was able successfully to fulfil the historical tasks of great significance entrusted to it. People who were erstwhile oppressed have become masters of their own destiny. The Tsarist empire was suppressed; this empire was formerly the prison of many nations and at the same time was enslaved by a handful of cosmopolitan financiers. The people were no longer the playthings, the slaves, the cannon fodder of rival imperialists. The toiling masses wiped out the wretchedness of bourgeois Russia where, as in other countries, the labouring people had suffered under the dreadful yoke of the capitalists and landlords; they were the creators of all wealth but were kept in misery and ignorance — both are the atrocious and age-long fate of the overwhelming majority of mankind. For the first time in human history, the working people started to build a society without class exploitation and national oppression — a socialist society. With their enthusiasm in labour, high consciousness, ever growing labour efficiency and with boundless faithfulness to their own cause, that of their children, and of their brothers who still suffer in slavery, the Soviet people have transformed their age-old dreams of happiness into a dazzling reality on a sixth of the earth.

The October Revolution and the building of socialism in the Soviet Union have considerably increased the revolutionary forces of the working class in the capitalist countries. The labouring peoples of many European and Asian countries have followed the example set by the Russian revolutionary proletariat.

In a short space of history, socialism has become a world system, now embracing twelve contries with more than 900 million people.

The October Revolution has shattered the fetters of imperialism, destroyed its foundation and inflicted on it a deadly blow. Like a thunderbolt, it has stirred up the Asian peoples from their centuries-old slumbers. It has opened up for them the revolutionary anti-imperialist era, the era of national liberation.

The Soviet Union is the strongest and most powerful bulwark of progress, democracy and peace. Its invincible and constantly developing strength and its consistent peace policy constitute the firmest guarantee for the independence of all nations, big and small. The Soviet Union has always made worthy efforts and has tabled practical proposals for arms reduction. It has persistently struggled for the suppression of nuclear and thermonuclear weapons which are threatening all nations. It has many a time asked other states to adopt collective security systems aimed at safeguarding peace in Europe and Asia. It has always upheld the five principles of peaceful co-existence and has endeavoured to make these five principles the basis of international relations between countries throughout the world.

The Soviet Union constantly shows loyalty to international solidarity, sympathises with and supports the struggle for liberation of all oppressed nations. All countries of the East, whatever their state or social regime, are deeply grateful to the Soviet Union for its peace policy and its proletarian internationalism. These policies inspire the peoples of the East with an ever-growing confidence in the great socialist ideology.

The power brought into being by the October Revolution set an example of genuine freedom and friendship between nations.

As early as 1913, Lenin said: "Everywhere in Asia a strong democratic movement is growing, spreading and being consolidated. There the bourgeoisie is still siding with the people to fight the reactionaries. Hundreds of millions of people are rising up in life, light and liberty . . . All young Asia, that is, hundreds of millions of toiling masses in Asia have a staunch ally — the proletariat of all civilised countries. No force on earth can prevent its victory, which will liberate all the peoples of Europe as well as of Asia."

In 1919, at the Eastern Communists' Congress, Lenin said: "A task is laid before you here, which has previously not been laid before the communists of the whole world: basing yourselves on the general theory and practice of communism, you must, in adapting yourselves to specific conditions which do not exist in the European countries, learn how to apply this theory and this practice to the conditions when the peasantry forms the basic masses, when it is necessary to settle the task of struggle not against capitalism but against mediaeval vestiges."

Dealing a telling blow at the common enemy — imperialism — the October Revolution has brought to the Eastern peoples assistance of a decisive character; it has given them the example of the liberation struggles of the countries once oppressed by Tsarism.

The October Revolution has brought to the people of all nations the right to decide their own fate and the practical means to implement this right. It is well known that Lenin attached particular importance to the recognition of the right of all nations to secession and to build up independent states. Opposing Bukharin's theories, Lenin resolutely demanded that this right should be inserted into the Party's Political programme expounded at the VIIIth Congress in March, 1919. The Soviet Union of the October Revolution recognised the independence of Mongolia and Finland, which seceded to build up independent states. Of course, for the formerly oppressed nations, the right to secession does not signify the obligation to secede from a state where the people have overthrown the oppressors. On the contrary, it creates conditions for a voluntary alliance between free nations on the basis of complete equality of interests. It was on this basis that in December 1922, the Union of the Soviet Socialist Republics was founded — a great example of a multi-national socialist state built on friendship, mutual confidence and good co-operation between nationalities.

Today, in the Soviet Union, thanks to the friendly assistance of the Russian people, the nationalities formerly oppressed by the Tsarist regime have reached an unprecedented level of development. They are able to establish their own institutions, restore and develop their own culture in their own language. All Soviet citizens, regardless of nationality and race, enjoy complete equality and the same freedoms, not only written on paper but actually ensured. This is a situation unknown to the workers of even the most democratic bourgeois countries where acknowledged freedoms guaranteed by law are cancelled out by actual social conditions. That is why the freedoms enjoyed by the Soviet peoples have fired the hearts of millions of people who are living under colonialist oppression. The ruling circles in the imperialist countries are stifling the most elementary freedoms of the colonial and dependent peoples, while inscribing the ironic legend "Liberty, Equality, Fraternity" in jails and places where tortures are carried out.

All the Soviet nationalities are animated by an ardent and genuine patriotism — a patriotism inseparable from proletarian internationalism.

For the first time in history, the national question has been solved by the victorious working class in a satisfactory way, on the basis of Marxist-Leninist principles.

Marxism-Leninism has elaborated a just and complete theory of anti-imperialist national revolution. The era of monopoly capitalism is also one where a few great powers, swayed by a handful of financiers, exercise their domination over dependent and semi-dependent countries; therefore the liberation of the oppressed countries and peoples has become an integral part of the proletarian revolution.

Hence there arises in the first place the possibility of and the need for a close fighting alliance between the colonial peoples and the proletariat of the imperialist countries, to triumph over the common enemy. The revolutionary struggle of the workers of the capitalist countries directly helps the oppressed peoples free themselves, by striking direct blows at the heart of the oppressors; this was vividly demonstrated by the October Revolution which has overthrown the power of the exploiters in Russia and resolutely abolished the oppressive colonial policy of the Tsarist regime and the Russian bourgeois class. In its turn, the revolutionary struggle of colonial and semi-colonial peoples directly helps the proletariat of the capitalist countries in their fight against the ruling classes to free themselves from the yoke of capitalism. The unity of the anti-imperialist struggle carries the certainty of victory for all colonial and semi-colonial peoples and for the proletariat in the capitalist countries.

Therefore, the national question can no longer be viewed from an abstract and isolated point of view. Marxism-

Leninism has shown that national movements, effectively directed against imperialism, unfailingly contribute to the general revolutionary struggle; that national claims and national movements must not be estimated according to their strictly local political and social character in a narrow-minded way, but according to the part they play against the imperialist forces in the world. Marxism-Leninism has unmasked bourgeois democracy, which dissimulated behind sermons on the abstract "equality" between nations to conceal the oppression and exploitation of the great number of nations in the world by a handful of imperialist countries. Marxism-Leninism makes a clear distinction, between "oppressed, dependent and subject nations, and the oppressing, exploiting and sovereign nations . . ."

To handle in a scientific way those problems on the basis of Marxism-Leninism and of the inexhaustible theoretical and practical experiences of the Soviet Union, at the same time to pay heed to the peculiarities of all dependent countries, is of great importance for the study of political lines, to continue the development of the national liberation movement and the organisation of social forces in the revolutions for liberation in the Eastern countries. In 1923, Lenin wrote on the dependent countries as follows: "Our European philistines never even dream that the subsequent revolutions — in Oriental countries, which possess much vaster populations and a much vaster diversity of social conditions, will undoubtedly display even greater peculiarities than the Russian revolution."

During the course of the emancipation struggle of the Eastern peoples, the Marxist-Leninist principles in the question of colonial liberation have been triumphantly confirmed. The October Revolution provided strong impetus for this struggle, and the existence of the Soviet Union constituted an important historic factor which helped that struggle develop rapidly.

The revolution in the colonial and semi-colonial countries is a national democratic revolution. To make it successful, it is possible and necessary to form a very wide national front, uniting all social strata and classes longing for liberation from colonialist yoke. In particular, one should bear in mind that the role played by the bourgeoisie in colonial and dependent countries in general is not similar to that played by the bourgeoisie in capitalist countries. The national bourgeoisie can be won to participate actively in the national-democratic revolution.

The revolution in the colonial and semi-colonial countries is first and foremost a peasant revolution. It is inseparable from the antifeudal revolution. The alliance of the broad peasant masses with the working class is the fundamental base on which a wide and firm national front can be formed. Consequently, agrarian reform is a fundamental task of the national democratic revolution.

To lead the national revolution to victory and to cover the successive stages of the development of the national democratic state, the working class and its Party must take up their role of leading the revolution.

The revolution for liberation of the oppressed countries and the revolution of the proletariat of the oppressing countries must support each other. In the oppressing countries, the central task in the education of internationalism is to help the toiling people clearly understand the right of oppressed nationalities to secession and to found independent states, and in the oppressed countries this task consists in allying the various nationalities on a voluntary basis. Lenin said: "The situation which presents itself provides no other path leading to internationalism and the concord between peoples, no other path leading to this goal".

The October Revolution teaches us to unite closely the efforts of the world proletariat, of the oppressed peoples and other peace forces in the whole world to struggle against imperialism and war.

"Unless the proletariat and, following it, all the toiling masses of all countries and nations all over the world voluntarily strive for alliance and unity, victory over capitalism cannot be successfully accomplished", said Lenin. And he added: "In the last analysis, the outcome of the struggle will

119

be determined by the fact that Russia, India, China, etc. account for the overwhelming majority of the population of the globe. And it is precisely this majority that, during the past few years, has been drawn into the struggle for emancipation with extraordinary rapidity, so that in this respect there cannot be the slightest shadow of doubt as to what the final outcome of the world struggle will be. In this sense, the complete victory of socialism is fully and absolutely assured."

TALK AT A PRESS CONFERENCE AT RANGOON

(Extract, February 16, 1958)

From 1955 onwards, the Government of the Democratic Republic of Vietnam has sent repeated proposals to the South Vietnam authorities, to hold a consultative conference and discuss general elections for national reunification. We have made repeated proposals to restore normal relations in economic, cultural and social spheres, between the two zones. However, due to foreign interference, so far the Southern authorities have not answered us yet.

Our position of the problem of national reunification is very clear. We stand for the reunification of our Fatherland on the basis of independence and democracy, through peaceful means, as stipulated by the Geneva Agreement, without coercion from or annexation by any side on the other. We are always ready to meet the Southern authorities and start with them from a spirit of negotiation and mutual understanding to discuss on general elections for Vietnam's reunification. Nation-wide general elections will be organised on the principle of universal suffrage and equality by direct and secret ballot and under the supervision of the International Commission as provided for by the Geneva Agreement. The National Assembly will issue the Supreme Constitution of the State, which will effectively ensure the privileges of the deputies. A coalition government elected by the National Assembly will be set up to strengthen solidarity among various parties, strata, nationalities, zones. Taking into account the particularities differentiating the two zones, each region may issue suitable local laws and regulations, which do not run counter to the State general law. Pending national reunification competent authorities in both zones should work for mutual understanding between both zones, by restoring normal relations between them and guaranteeing all democratic freedoms to all organisations and individuals standing for peace, reunification and democracy. We consider that such a policy conforms to both sense and reason, because it is rooted in the legitimate aspirations of the whole Vietnamese people and from the realities in both zones and is in full keeping with the Geneva Agreement.

Vietnam is a monolithic bloc that nothing can divide. For centuries past, the Vietnamese people have built up their Fatherland and, from North to South, they have one common history, one language, one economy, together they rose to oppose colonialism. Now they will resolutely struggle for national reunification. The South Vietnam authorities should stop illegal introduction of arms and munitions in South Vietnam, refrain from terrorising patriotic people who stand for peace and reunification, and restore normal relations between the two zones; they should hold a consultative conference with the Government of the Democratic Republic of Vietnam to discuss on the general elections to reunify Vietnam as provided for by the Geneva Agreement.

With the Vietnamese people's tradition of solidarity and struggle, and thanks to the world people's sympathy and support, our struggle for national reunification will be certainly successful, because it is a just struggle.

OUR PARTY

*(Extracts from a Speech delivered on November 28, 1959 at
a Conference for the Study of the History of the Vietnam
Workers' Party)*

Before our Party was founded, there were in our country
three communist groups. In 1930 a meeting took place to
discuss their merging. Repression by the enemy was at its
fiercest. The delegates had to leave secretly for Hong Kong.
Feigning to attend a football match, we sat on the grass
and discussed. Finally it was agreed that three groups
should be amalgamated into a single Party, the Indochinese
Communist Party.

Our Party was born when the French colonialists were
carrying out fierce repression. Soon after its birth, it organised and led the most heroic struggle for the Nghe-Tinh
Soviet.

When it was twelve years old it organised the guerilla
movement to fight the French and Japanese.

Aged fifteen, it organised and led to success the August
Revolution.

From the age of seventeen, it led the Resistance War,
and at twenty-four it brought the Resistance War to victory.

After the restoration of peace, our Party led and organised our people to build socialism in the North, thus turning
it into a base of struggle for national reunification.

Thus in thirty years, our Party has led two revolutions,
the national democratic revolution and the socialist revolution. What made our Party win such victories?

In the beginning, Party members were very few and were
often arrested and imprisoned by the French colonialists.
But our Party constantly marched forward. When the
August Revolution took place, there were about 5,000
Party members, including those in jail. Less than 5,000

Party members have thus organised and led the uprisings of 24 million fellow-countrymen over the country to victory.

Why did our Party achieve such glorious successes? At that time, a revolutionary might carry out his work until the revolution triumphed, or be arrested, murdered. But the conviction that the Party would win final victory was unshakable, so when anyone was arrested he was immediately replaced by another, when anyone was killed, a hundred were ready to take over his task. Party members were strongly united, single-minded, and very close to the people. That is why, despite its small number, the Party has led the Revolution to victory.

Many Party members were of exemplary behaviour and revolutionary virtue. Comrade Minh Khai was twice condemned to death, and finally died very bravely. Comrades Tran Phu, Hoang Van Thu and many others have set examples of heroism.

Examples of heroism are also numerous in the Party members' activities. For instance, there were comrades who worked secretly in underground cellars for months, writing propaganda leaflets, translating books and newspapers. When they reappeared in the light of day their eyesight was weakened. There were comrades who, tortured by the enemy, lost consciousness several times, but did not say a word.

Our cadres and Party members are human beings, made of flesh and blood, but their faith in the Party, in the working class and in the force of the collective, makes them fight with determination until their last breath.

There were also young heroes like Young Trong, Young Sau, and many unknown heroes. That is why our Party became stronger and stronger.

In the Resistance War, there were in the ranks of our Party heroic comrades such as Phan Dinh Giot who blocked a loop-hole in the enemy fortress with his body so that our troops might advance, Vinh Dien who threw himself under the wheels of a gun carriage to stop its rolling downhill, and many others who pursued the enemy on an empty stomach for two or three days. These heroes of the Party, of the people, are heroes of the collective, they were imbued with the Party's revolutionary virtues. Only with revolutionary virtues can we lead the working class, organise and unite the masses to bring the Revolution and the Resistance War to victory.

At present, in building socialism, we have important and complex tasks to do. We have defeated the French colonialists and the feudal class, but we still have to fight against other dangerous enemies. These are poverty, hunger, backwardness.

We have started with a backward agriculture, a low standard of living. We have to struggle so that everyone in our country has enough food and clothes, work and leisure time, and receives education.

We have favourable conditions to build socialism. Our country has "forests of gold and seas of silver", our people are industrious. The brotherly countries are giving us aid. But there are also difficulties such as flood, drought, the low level of general education and technique.

As a whole, our cadres and Party members are good ones, faithful to the Revolution. If we struggle with determination we shall certainly overcome these difficulties. Of course, political consciousness is indispensable, a Party member must know about politics, must study politics. But general education and technique are necessary to handle machines which are becoming more and more complex. We are still weak in this field. In the factories of the Soviet Union many workers have finished their tenth form. But how many among the cadres here have finished their tenth form? So we have to learn much, we should endeavour to learn. Otherwise, we would not make progress. If we do not progress, we regress. As society progresses, there are more things to do, more complex machines. If we do not study, we shall lag behind, and if we lag behind we shall be rejected, through our own fault.

Is that right? If it is, you should endeavour to raise your cultural and professional level.

In our Party not a few comrades are conceited, they are

overbearing and self-satisfied because they have been engaged for many years in revolutionary activities. It is a good
thing to have engaged for a long time in revolutionary work,
but we should always be modest and endeavour to study
to progress unceasingly. Society progresses unceasingly. To
build socialism in the North, to make of the latter a base
for the struggle to reunify the country, we should endeavour
to study.

In our Party, many have set examples of bravery in face
of danger and sacrifice, because they believe in the Party,
in the Revolution and in the future of the working class
and of the Fatherland. At present, in the persistent struggle
against the American imperialists and the Diem clique, our
fellow-countrymen in the South are also displaying outstanding heroism.

In the North, all the labour heroes and model workers,
responding to the appeal by the Party, have been toiling
selflessly for the people and for the working class. They do
not think of personal gain and losses. They enthusiastically
do what the Party wants them to do, endeavouring to surpass the set target. That too is heroism.

We, Party members, are very ordinary people because we
are the sons of the working class, of the working people,
we are nothing but faithful to the proletarian class and
determined to struggle for the people. The fact that we are
very ordinary people makes our Party very great. Apart
from the interests of the Fatherland, of the working class
and of the people, our Party knows no other interest.

Yesterday's newspapers related the story of a militia-man
named Tran Van Tan, a Workers' Party member. He was
entrusted with the task of getting a quantity of timber,
together with some comrades. There was a storm and their
raft threatened to break up several times. Braving danger,
comrade Tan plunged into the river to repair the raft. When
the raft arrived at its destination, it was found that a number
of logs were missing. Comrade Tan volunteered to go and
look for them, and he brought back all of them after two or
three days. A militiaman is a man of ordinary position.

To get timber is an ordinary task. But to overcome all difficulties, to fulfil one's task, is heroism.

At present, in the countryside, a heated discussion is going on: *which way to follow, that of individualism or that of collectivism?*

Why is our Party strong and becoming stronger and stronger? Because our Party practises *collectivism*. Every Party member should do likewise. But a number of comrades have not been completely won to collectivism; individualism among them is still prevailing. For example in the question of remuneration they have shown discontent and jealousy. They want to do easy jobs and avoid hard ones. Those comrades do not remember that during the period of secret Party activities, during the Resistance War, and at present, the heroes and the model workers did not struggle and make sacrifices for any remuneration, position or rank.

The close allocation of work in the Party and the State is like clockwork. The hands of the clock and the spring are two different parts but they act in close unity. None of the parts of the clock can be done without. Likewise in our society, our Party is a closeknit collective which does not allow individualism. Individualism is the source of many evils. Everyone, whatever his work or his position may be, is important. Any work that is useful to the Party, to the Revolution, is honourable.

The individualists cater for their personal interests only, not for the collective's interests. They want to enjoy material privileges, they never volunteer for work. That is not good. With individualism there can be no enthusiasm, no progress.

Our Party is a great collective which is united in thought and in action. Every Party member must defend the Party and the Party's policies.

Has our Party shortcomings? It has. To transform the old society into a new one is no easy thing. It is like demolishing an old house and building a new palace. In building the new palace, we cannot avoid breaking a few bricks, scattering sawdust, etc. Likewise in building socialism, some shortcomings and mistakes are inevitable. But whenever it makes a mistake, the Party courageously admits it and resolutely corrects it.

Our Party has a very effective means to make its members progress, and the Party become stronger and stronger: *self-criticism and criticism*. Lenin has said: Only two categories of people are free from mistakes: the foetus in the womb and the dead in their coffins. Action is seldom free from mistakes. But when we make mistakes, we should frankly criticise ourselves, welcome criticisms and resolutely correct our mistakes. *Individualism* makes one fear self-criticism and criticism, prevents one from resolutely correcting one's mistakes. Thus it makes one regress instead of progressing.

In a word, our Party has been struggling heroically for the last thirty years and has won glorious victories. At present, it has to continue the struggle to reunify the country. In this struggle we have many advantages. But we also meet with many difficulties. If every cadre, every Party member fulfils his duties, fosters and enhances the spirit of collectivism, gets rid of individualism, and closely studies politics, general education and technical knowledge, we shall certainly overcome all difficulties, and brilliantly fulfil our duties.

Lastly, I trust you will remember all this and put it into practice. At present, we have over four hundred thousand Party members and over six hundred thousand Labour youths, a strong government, a most heroic army, and our people are showing great enthusiasm. Furthermore, our country is a member of the great socialist family headed by the great Soviet Union. Therefore, if our cadres and Party members fulfil their duties, closely study politics, general education and technical knowledge, we shall certainly succeed.

I wish you continuous progress.

THE DRAFT LAW ON MARRIAGE AND THE FAMILY

(October, 1959)

There are people who think that as a bachelor I may not have a perfect knowledge of this question. Though I have no family of my own, yet I have a very big family — the working class throughout the world and the Vietnamese people. From that broad family I can judge and imagine the small one.

At present, our entire people want socialist construction. What is to be done to build socialism?

Production must certainly be increased as much as possible. To increase production there must be much labour-power which can be obtained satisfactorily only by emancipating the women's labour power.

Women make up half of society. If they are not liberated, half of society is not freed.

If women are not emancipated only half of socialism is built.

It is correct to take a keen interest in the family; many families constitute the society. A good society makes a good family and vice versa. The core of the society is the family. It is precisely to build up socialism that due attention must be paid to this core.

"Living in concord, husband and wife may empty the East sea", as the proverb says.

To enjoy concord in matrimonial life, marriage must be based on genuine love.

The law on marriage to be presented to the National Assembly is a revolution, an integral part of the socialist revolution.

Therefore we should adopt the proletarian stand to understand it. It is not correct if our understanding is based on feudal, bourgeois or petty-bourgeois stand.

The law on marriage aims at emancipating women, that is at freeing half of society. The emancipation of the women must be carried out simultaneously with the extirpation of feudal and bourgeois thinking in men.

As for themselves, women should not wait until the directives of the Government and the Party free them but they must rely upon themselves and struggle.

The Party must give this law leadership from its preparation to its presentation and execution, because this is a revolution. The leadership by the Party means that all cadres and Party members must apply this law strictly and lead all Youth and Women's organisations resolutely and correctly to put it into effect.

The execution of this law is:

— on the one hand, easy because our people have received the Party education and have made much progress;

— and on the other, has many difficulties because of the long-standing and deeply rooted old habits and traditions among the people. That is why everything is not over with the promulgation of this law but *long-term propaganda and education needs to be carried on to obtain good results.*

I hope that all of you will do your best, be patient, have a thorough knowledge of this law and carry it out satisfactorily. In particular, you must be very careful because this law exerts great influence on *the future of the family, the society and the nation.*

REPORT ON THE DRAFT AMENDED CONSTITUTION

(Extracts from Report delivered to the National Assembly, December 18, 1959.)

At its 6th session, the National Assembly decided upon amending the 1946 Constitution and setting up a Committee for Amendment of the Constitution to present a draft to the National Assembly.

The drafting of the amendment to the Constitution has undergone a long process of preparation and careful study. Following completion of the first draft in July 1958, we submitted it for discussion by high-ranking and middle cadres in the army, civil, administrative and Party offices. After these discussions, the draft was improved, and on April 1st, 1959, it was made known to the entire people for discussion and constructive suggestions. These discussions lasted four consecutive months. Everywhere in offices, factories, schools and other people's organisations, in the cities and the countryside, the study and discussions of the draft Constitution proceeded in an enthusiastic atmsophere and became a broad mass movement with the participation of all sections of the people. In the press, the discussions were also lively and fruitful. The Committee for Amendment of the Constitution has received many letters sending in the views of individuals and groups, including letters from our dear compatriots in the South and abroad.

The views contributed by the people have been carefully studied and debated by the Committee for Amendment of the Constitution and, on the basis of this, we have improved the draft for a second time.

We are advancing to a socialist economy. Along with these successes class relations in North Vietnamese society have changed. The feudal landlord class has been overthrown. The working-class is growing day by day and is strengthening its leadership over the State. The peasantry is embarking on the co-operative path. The worker-peasant alliance is further strengthened. The revolutionary intellectuals are contributing an active part to national construction. The national bourgeois, generally speaking, accept the socialist transformation. Various sections of our people are united more closely within the ranks of the National United Front. Compared with 1946, when the first Constitution of our country was adopted, the situation in present-day North Vietnam has undergone very big and good changes.

While the North is advancing to socialism, in the South the U. S. imperialists and their henchmen undermine the Geneva Agreements and refuse to hold the consultative conference on general elections to reunify the country. They are enforcing an extremely cruel and autocratic policy, extorting the property of the people, repressing and persecuting them in the most barbarous manner. They seek to perpetuate the division of our country and turn the South into a colony and a military base of the U. S. imperialists, in an attempt to provoke a new war in Indo-China.

But our compatriots in the South are very heroic; the struggle there is steadily preserved and developed. Our southern compatriots demand an improvement in their life and national reunification; they oppose oppression, exploitation and American "aid", repression and massacre, military reinforcements and war preparations.

North Vietnam, advancing to socialism, powerfully stimulates the patriotic movement in South Vietnam. Our southern compatriots are constantly looking towards the North and our government, and raise their confidence in the cause of national reunification.

In short, the Vietnamese revolution has moved on to a new stage. We have new tasks to achieve. The conditions in both the country and the world are favourable to us.

The 1946 Constitution — the first democratic Constitution of our country — conformed to the situation and the revolutionary task of that period. It has completed its mission. It is no longer compatible with the new situation and the present-day new revolutionary tasks. That is why we must amend the Constitution.

The draft amended Constitution clearly records the great successes of our people in the past years and clearly outlines the new revolutionary tasks in the new historic period.

I present a summary of some main points in the content of the draft Constitution as follows:

1. Character of the Vietnam Democratic Republican State.

The character of the State is the fundamental question in the Constitution. This is the question of class content of power. In whose hands is the power and whose rights does it serve? This question determines the overall content of the Constitution.

Our State, established after the August Revolution, was already a people's democratic State, led by the working-class. Now, the Preamble of the draft amended Constitution again points out:

"Our State is a people's democratic state based on the worker-peasant alliance and led by the working-class."

In order to build socialism and struggle for the achievement of national reunification, we must unceasingly strengthen the leadership of the working-class in the people's democratic State.

The worker-peasant alliance is the foundation of the Vietnam Democratic Republican State. The peasantry constitutes a very big productive force and at the same time a very great revolutionary force. In the national people's democratic revolution, the peasants have energetically followed the Party in the rising side by side with the working-class to overthrow imperialism and feudalism. At present they are enthusiastically joining the agricultural co-operative movement. This is due to the active revolutionary spirit of our peasants and due to the persistent and continued education of the Party and the working-class. Therefore, in building socialism, our State strives to help the peasantry and consolidate the worker-peasant alliance.

The working-class unites with handicraftsmen and small traders because they are working people; they willingly take the path of co-operation, approve of and support the socialist revolution.

The socialist revolution is intimately linked with scientific and technical development and the cultural development of the people. Our intellectuals contributed a valuable part to the resistance. They have been constantly assisted by the Party to make progress. That is why they want socialism. The working-class closely unites with the intelligentsia to help it serve the revolution and socialism.

Under the leadership of the working class, the Vietnamese national bourgeois have supported the national people's democratic revolution. Since the restoration of peace they have contributed their part to economic rehabilitation. At present we have the condition to transform them along socialist lines. In the Northern part of our country, the socialist economic forces are definitely superior to the capitalist economic forces. We have the people's power. The revolutionary struggle of the working masses is growing powerfully. The national bourgeoisie is ready to accept transformation to contribute to national construction and the building of socialism.

Our country is a united multi-national country. All nationalities living on Vietnam territory are equal in rights and duties.

All the fraternal nationalities in our country are bound together by an affection of kith-and-kin; we have lived on a common territory and experienced a long history of common labour and struggle in building our beautiful Fatherland.

Imperialism and feudalism have deliberately undermined the solidarity and equality between the nationalities, sown discord among them and carried out a policy of "divide and rule". Our Party and Government have constantly called on the nationalities to remove all discord engineered by imperialism and feudalism and to unite closely on the basis of equality in rights and duties. The minority nationals have, side by side with their brothers the majority nationals, fought against their common enemies, and brought the August Revolution and the resistance to success. Since the restoration of peace, our State has helped the brotherly nationalities to achieve further progress in the economic, cultural and social fields. The Viet Bac and the Thai-Meo Autonomous regions have been established. Closely united under the leadership of the Party and the State, the nationalities are enthusiastically taking part in the emulation movement for national construction.

Our policy on nationalities is aimed at achieving equality between the nationalities to advance together to socialism. Autonomous regions may be established in areas where minority nationals live in compact communities.

2. *General line of advance to socialism*

For nearly one hundred years, Vietnam was a colonial and semifeudal country. The economy was very backward and composed of many complicated sectors; production was not developed and the people's material and cultural living standards were low. To change this situation of poverty, North Vietnam must advance to socialism.

Article 9 of the draft amended Constitution points out that the line of advance to socialism is: "The Democratic Republic of Vietnam is advancing step by step from people's democracy to socialism by developing and transforming the national economy along socialist lines, transforming its backward economy into a socialist economy with modern industry and agriculture and advanced science and technology. The economic policy of the Democratic Republic of Vietnam is to continuously develop production with the aim of constantly raising the material and cultural standards of the people."

There are at present in our country the following forms of ownership of the means of production:

— Ownership by the State, that is ownership by the entire people;

— Ownership by the co-operatives, that is collective ownership by the working people,

— Ownership by individual working people,

— A small proportion of the means of production is owned by the capitalists.

The aim of our regime is to eliminate the forms of non-socialist ownership, to turn the present economy composed of many complicated sectors into a single economy based on the system of public ownership by the people and of collective ownership.

Under article 12 of the draft amended Constitution, the State economic sector is a form of ownership by the whole people; it leads the national economy, and the State must ensure priority for its development.

Under article 13, the co-operative economic sector is a form of collective ownership by the working people; the State particularly encourages, guides and helps its development.

We must develop the State economic sector to create the material foundation for socialism and stimulate socialist transformation.

Agricultural production is the main driving wheel of the socialist transformation in the North. Past experiences have shown that agricultural co-operation in our country must pass through the forms of work-exchange teams and agricultural producers' co-operatives. This is very necessary. If we steadily develop step by step the work-exchange teams and the co-operatives, agricultural production will certainly be successful.

— Towards handicraftsmen and other individual workers, the State protects their right to ownership of their means of production, actively guides and helps them to improve their ways of earning their livelihood, and encourages them to organise agricultural producers' co-operatives in accordance with the principle of voluntariness.

— Towards capitalist traders and industrialists, the State does not cancel their right to ownership of the means of production and other property but actively guides them to act in line with the interests of the State and the people's welfare and in keeping with the State economic plan. At the same time, the State encourages and helps them to transform themselves along socialist line through the forms of joint state and private ownership and other forms of transformation.

Under article 10 of the draft amended Constitution, the State leads economic activities according to a unified plan. The State makes use of its organs and relies on the trade unions and the co-operatives and other organisations of the working people to map and carry out its economic plans.

Since the restoration of peace and beginning with the economic restoration, we have gradually taken the economy in the North along the path of planned development. We have had the three-year programme for economic rehabilitation (1955—1957). At present we are carrying out the three-year plan for initial development of the economy and culture and preparing conditions to carry out our first five-year plan. The three-year plan aims particularly at promoting the socialist transformation of the economic sector of private ownership by the peasants, handicraftsmen and other individual working people and the economic sector of capitalist ownership; at the same time it enlarges and reinforces the economic sector of State ownership, sti mulates the economic development along socialist lines.

3. Organisation of the Vietnam Democratic Republican State.

In order to fulfil well the revolutionary tasks, our State must develop the democratic rights and political activities of the entire people, to promote their ardour and creativeness, helping all citizens of Vietnam to take part effectively in managing State affairs, to endeavour to build socialism and struggle for national reunification.

Our revolutionary regime has been established over nearly fifteen years. The 1946 Constitution established the People's Assembly and People's Councils at various levels. The National Assembly is a People's Council of the entire country. There are People's Councils of the localities. The National Assembly and the People's Councils are composed of representatives elected by the people through universal suffrage. The National Assembly decides on the most important affairs of the State. The People's Councils decide on the most important affairs of the localities.

During the resistance, the National Assembly together with the Government united and guided our people, bringing the patriotic and anti-imperialist war to glorious victory. The National Assembly adopted the law on land reform aimed at completing the anti-feudalist revolution. In the localities, the People's Councils contributed to the mobilisation of the people in taking an active part in the anti-imperialist and anti-feudalist revolution.

Since the restoration of peace, the National Assembly has adopted the three-year programme for economic rehabilitation, the three-year plan for initial development of the economy and culture, the policies on economic development and transformation along the socialist lines and the laws on democratic freedoms and so on. These are most important problems relating to State affairs and the people's livelihood.

Under article 4 of the draft amended Constitution, all the powers in the Democratic Republic of Vietnam belong to the people. The people exercise their authority through the National Assembly and the People's Councils at various levels which are elected by the people and responsible to the people.

Our electoral system is democratic and develops solidarity among the entire people. All citizens from the age of 18 upward have the right to elect, and from the age of 21 upward have the right to stand for election. Elections will be held on the principle of universal, equal, direct and secret suffrage.

The people have the right to dismiss the deputies to the National Assembly and the deputies to the People's Councils should these deputies show themselves unworthy of the people's trust. This principle guarantees the people's right of control over their representatives.

Article 6 of the draft amended Constitution stipulates that it is the duty of all organs of the State to rely upon the people, keep close contact with the people, carefully listen to the people's opinions and accept the people's supervision.

The National Assembly is the supreme authoritative organ of the State. The People's Councils are State authoritative organs in the localities.

The National Assembly elects the President of the State, the Standing Committee of the National Assembly and the Council of Ministers. The Council of Ministers is the organ enacting the laws and decisions of the National Assembly and the highest administrative organ of the State. It is responsible to the National Assembly and has to report to it on its work. In the period between two sessions of the National Assembly, the Council of Ministers is responsible and has to report to the National Assembly Standing Committee on its work.

The National Assembly is the only organ having legislative power. The most important affairs of the State on a national scale are decided upon by the National Assembly.

The People's Councils elect the administrative committee at various levels. Administrative committees at various levels are executive organs of the People's Councils. They are responsible to the People's Councils and have to report to them on their work. At the same time they are placed under the direct leadership of the administrative committees at a higher level and under the unified leadership of the Council of Ministers.

The most important affairs in the localities are decided upon by the People's Councils.

Our economic and social system aims at fully achieving the democratic rights of the people. On the basis of increasing development of the socialist economy, gradual elimination of capitalist exploitation, the material and cultural standards of the people will be improved day by day. Therefore our people will have all the conditions necessary for taking part effectively in managing the State.

Article 4 of the draft amended Constitution clearly stipulates that the principle of organisation of our State i democratic centralism. The National Assembly, the People' Councils, the Central Government and other State organ all follow the principle of democratic centralism.

Our State ensures development of democracy to the highest degree, this is because of its character as a State of the people. Only through the highest development o democracy are all forces of the people mobilised to take the revolution forward. At the same time the highest centralism must be ensured to lead the people in building socialism

4. Basic rights and duties of citizens.

The draft amended Constitution clearly stipulates the basic rights and duties of citizens in our country. These stipulations demonstrate the genuinely democratic character of our regime.

The capitalists often boast that their Constitution guarantees the rights of the individual, the right to democratic liberties and the interests of all citizens. But in reality, only the bourgeoisie enjoys the rights recorded in the Constitution. The working people do not really enjoy democratic freedoms; they are exploited during all their life and have to bear all the heavy burden to serve the interests of the exploiting class.

The capitalists often slander that our socialist regime does not respect the personal interests of the citizens. But in reality, only our regime is really able to serve the interests of the people, first and foremost the working people, guarantee all the people's interests and broadening democracy, thus enabling the people to really take part in the management of the State. That is why the people in our country display

ll their energies to fulfil their duties as the masters of the
ountry, to build socialism and make our country stronger
nd our people prosperous.

The draft amended Constitution clearly points out: the
itizens of the Democratic Republic of Vietnam have:

— the right to work,
— the right to rest,
— the right to study,
— the right to personal liberty,
— freedom of opinion, of the press, assembly, organi-
ation, to hold demonstrations,
— freedom of religious belief, to adhere or not to adhere
o any religion,
— the right to elect and stand for election, etc.

All citizens are equal before the law. Women enjoy equal
ights with men in every respect: political, economic, cul-
ural, social and in the family. The State pays particular
ttention to moral, intellectual and physical education of
he youth.

In view of the character of our State, of our economic and
ocial system, the State not only recognises the interests of
he citizens but also guarantees the necessary material
onditions for them to enjoy these interests effectively.

The State guarantees democratic freedoms to the citizens,
ut strictly prohibits any misuse of these freedoms to
nfringe on the interests of the State and the people, as
learly stipulated in article 38 of the draft amended Con-
titution.

In our regime the interests of the State, the collective
nd the individual are basically at one with each other.
Therefore, while enjoying the rights of the State and the
ollective all citizens must consciously fulfil their duties
owards the State and the collective.

The citizens have the duty to respect the Constitution,
he law, labour regulations, public order and the rules of
ocial life. The citizens have the duty to respect public
property, to pay taxes according to the law, to do military
ervice to defend the Fatherland.

141

Only in a socialist system can the interests of the individual and the State as well as that of the collective b
at one. That is why only a socialist Constitution can encour
age the citizens to enthusiastically fulfil their duty towar
the society and the Fatherland.

Thirty Years of Activity of the Vietnam Workers' Party

(Article in "World Marxist Review", No. 2, 1960)

Our Party is celebrating its thiertieth anniversary. We would like to cast a retrospective glance at the path traversed and the battles fought and won, and to generalise the valuable experiences accumulated in order correctly to determine the revolutionary tasks of the present stage and of the immediate future.

Just as the changes that have taken place in our country are inseparable from international developments, so the strengthening of our Party is inseparable from the growth of the fraternal Parties. The Great October Socialist Revolution, which made a big breach in the walls of capitalism, opened to the world proletariat and the oppressed peoples the way to liberation. In 1919, under Lenin's leadership, genuine revolutionaries founded the Third International. Communist Parties were formed in many countries. Under the impact of the October Revolution and with the direct help of the Communist Parties of China and France, Marxism-Leninism penetrated the iron curtain lowered by French colonialism and reached Viet Nam.

From 1924 on, the revolutionary movement in our country began to grow; the working class, which fought first for economic demands, soon went over to political struggle. The union of Marxist-Leninist theory with the working class and patriotic movement led to the *formation, early in 1930, of the Communist Party of Indo-China* (since March 1951 the Vietnam Workers' Party).

This event, which marked a turning point in the Vietnamese Revolution, showed that the working class had matured and was capable of heading the revolutionary struggle.

Our Party passed through several important stages: underground activity, revolutionary struggle ending in the August Revolution, the years of the victorious patriotic war. Now the northern part of the country has entered the stage of socialist revolution, that of the struggle for the national reunification and the completion of the democratic revolution throughout the land.

During its almost fifteen years of underground activities the Party was savagely persecuted by the French colonialists, whom it fought relentlessly. The jails, including the penal prisons on the island of Poulo Condor, in Lao Bao and in Son La, were filled with communists. Many Party cadres and members died the death of the brave in the struggle. But we firmly believed in the ultimate victory of the Party and the Revolution, and our ranks continued to grow and gain in strength.

Ever since its inception the Party has held aloft the banner of the national democratic revolution and has led the national liberation movement. At that time the feudal class capitulated to the imperialists, while the bourgeoisie, being weak and fearing economic destruction, sought to come to terms with imperialism. Despite the ferment in their midst the petty bourgeois sections had come to a dead end. The working class alone, as the most revolutionary class, kept up the struggle against the colonialists. Equipped with advanced revolutionary theory and the experience of the international proletarian movement, it proved itself the most able leader, one worthy of the confidence of the people.

Educated in the spirit of Marxism-Leninism, the Communist Party pursued a correct revolutionary policy. As early as 1930 it enunciated the tasks of the bourgeois-democratic revolution: *the struggle against the imperialists and feudal lords*, the winning of national independence and the transfer of the land to the peasants. This programme was fully in keeping with the aspirations of the peasants, who comprised the majority of the people. In this way our Party succeeded in uniting large revolutionary forces around the working class, while the parties of the other classes either met with fiasco or found themselves isolated. The leading role of our Party of the working class was confirmed, and its prestige grew.

Shortly after its formation the Party organised and led the *mass movement for Soviets in the Nghe An and Ha Tinh provinces*. The workers and peasants in these provinces threw off the imperialist and feudal yoke, established worker-peasant-soldier rule, and proclaimed democratic liberties for the working people.

Although the movement was savagely crushed, it will testify for all time to the heroism and the will to fight of the working masses. It promoted the growth of the forces which subsequently accomplished the August Revolution.

When, in 1936, the menace of fascism and the threat of world war became obvious, our Party aligned itself with the international anti-fascist democratic front and the Popular Front in France. It initiated the *struggle for the formation in Indo-China of a democratic front against fascism and colonial reaction*, and led the mass actions to win democratic liberties and better conditions. This movement embraced millions of people, awakening them to the political struggle. The prestige of the Communist Party mounted among the working people.

Shortly after the beginning of the Second World War, Vietnam was occupied by the Japense aggressors, who sought to dominate the country; for which purpose they aligned themselves with the French colonialists. The Party changed its tactics in time. *Viet Minh* (League for the Independence of Viet Nam) and *mass organisations of national salvation* were established in 1941. With a view to rallying all the patriotic forces in a single anti-fascist and anti-colonial bloc, the Party temporarily withdrew the slogan for agrarian revolution, confining itself to demands for lower rents and lower interest rates, for confiscation of the land belonging to the imperialists and traitors and handing it over to the peasants. In this way we sought to unite all forces in the struggle against the imperialists and their stooges, to drawt he patriotic landlords into it and to extend the National Front for the Salvation of the country.

The Party's policy furthered the growth of the revolutionary movement. Resistance bases were set up, and the first units of the Vietnamese Army of Liberation formed. The Communist Party started *guerilla warfare against the Japanese invaders*, and played an active part in the international anti-fascist struggle.

This made it possible, immediately after the Soviet Army had smashed fascism, to carry out the *national uprising for the conquest of power*. This was in fact the victorious August Revolution of 1945, which gave birth to the Democratic Republic of Vietnam.

In 1945 our Party, which had been formed from a few Marxist study groups, had only about 5,000 members, many of whom were in prison. But it had been steeled in hard battles and although numerically small, it was able to unite the people and lead the uprising to victory — the first great victory won by Marxism-Leninism in a colony.

Not long after the August Revolution the French Government violated the agreements it had signed with our Republic and unleashed an aggressive war.

At that time the country was in dire straits. We had not got over the famine caused by the policy pursued by French imperialism and Japanese fascism. The enemy had considerable land, sea and air forces equipped with modern weapons. We had only a few newly-formed, poorly quipped infantry regiments with little combat experience. But the Party decided to organise resistance. Heading the patriotic struggle to preserve the democratic republic, it simultaneously carried out a number of important social and economic measures. When the resistance became widespread, we took the course of *carrying out an agrarian reform*, and mobilised the people under the slogan of "Land to the tillers". This was a correct policy. The Resistance forces, joined by increasing numbers of peasants, grew rapidly and began to win one victory after another.

Our country had been under the French colonialist yoke for some eighty years. In the nine years of the patriotic war a real army had grown out of the first few detachments. The people rallied in an indissoluble union. The first small regular units, guerilla detachments and the people's militia expanded into an army of heroes, confident of victory and ready for any ordeals.

The unity and self-sacrifice of the army and the people won the historic victory of Dien Bien Phu in May 1954. The French colonialist troops never recovered from this defeat, and were compelled to agree to a cease-fire. Agreements signed in Geneva brought about peace on the basis of the recognition of the independence, sovereignty and territorial integrity of the peoples of Indo-China.

For the first time in history a small colony had emerged the victor in single combat with a big colonial power. This was a victory not only of our people, but, simultaneously, a victory of the world forces of peace, democracy and socialism.

Once again Marxism-Leninism illuminated the path for the working class and the people, and led them to triumph in the struggle to save their country and safeguard the revolutionary gains.

After the restoration of peace, the country found itself temporarily divided into two parts. Socialism is being built in the liberated, northern part of Vietnam, while the imperialists and their underlings, now converting the South into an American colony and military base with the object of embroiling us in another civil war, are lording it in the South. The American imperialists and their stooges, the sworn enemies of the Vietnamese people, are brazenly violating the Geneva Agreements, putting roadblocks in the way of convening a consultative conference to arrange for free elections and the peaceful reunification of the country.

In this situation *two tasks* confront the Vietnamese revolution; first, the construction of socialism in North Vietnam, and second, the completion of the national-democratic revolution in the South. The fulfilment of these tasks will

147

strengthen peace and pave the way to reunification on the basis of independence and democracy.

This is how the Fifteenth Plenary Meeting of the Central Committee of the Vietnam Workers' Party defined the tasks facing the people: "Consolidation of the national unity of the people, vigorous action for the union of the country on the basis of independence and democracy, completion of the national-democratic revolution in South Vietnam, strengthening of all the forces in the North and leading it towards socialism, establishing a peaceful, unified, independent, democratic and prosperous state, safeguarding peace in Indo-China, in South-east Asia and throughout the world."

North Vietnam advances steadily along the socialist path. The feature of the transitional period in our economically backward agrarian country is *the direct advance towards socialism, by-passing the capitalist stage of development.*

The French imperialists left us an economy in a bad plight. Small peasant farming prevailed in the countryside. For all practical purposes there was no industry. Fifteen years of war had ruined the economy. The situation was worsened by the economic sabotage carried out by the colonialists before withdrawing from North Viet Nam.

In these conditions the cardinal task was to build the material and technical base of socialism, gradually to expand the national economy, develop a modern industry, agriculture and educational system. The reconstruction of the old and the creation of a new economy calls for constructive labour over a long period.

Between 1955 and 1957 the No. 1 problem was *rehabilitation*. It was necessary to restore agriculture and industry, to heal the wounds of war, stabilise the economy and improve living standards.

Thanks to the efforts of the people and the fraternal aid accorded us by the socialist camp, the rehabilitation was successfully completed by the end of 1957. The level of industrial and agricultural output was approximately that of 1939. Impressive results were achieved in raising food crops: North Vietnam, which in 1939 produced about 2,500,000 tons of paddy, harvested 4,000,000 tons in 1956.

This period witnessed radical changes in the production relations. The agrarian reform abolished the system of feudal land ownership and released the productive forces in the countryside. The cherished dream of 12,000,000 peasants, the dream that the land would be divided among them, had now come true. The economic monopoly of the imperialists was abolished. The State took control of the economic levers and began to build a socialist economy. Thanks to the generous aid rendered by the socialist states, primarily the Soviet Union and China, twenty-nine old industrial enterprises were reconstructed and fifty-five new ones built.

In many districts the peasants united into *mutual-aid teams*, embryonic forms of socialism. Experimental *agricultural co-operatives* were formed, and the handicraftsmen have joined in production groups.

Private industry and trade switched over to State capitalism working on government orders and using the raw materials provided by the State, supplying traders with the goods from the State-owned organisations, etc.

After the rehabilitation the Party mobilised the people for fulfilment of the Three-Year Plan (1958—60). This plan aims at reconstructing agriculture, handicraft production, industry and trade along socialist lines. It was agreed that the emphasis should be laid on socialist reconstruction and expansion of agriculture as the fundamental condition for the industrialisation of the country. Industry and foreign trade can expand only on the basis of a prospering socialist agriculture. When completed, the reconstruction of agriculture, as envisaged in the plan, will create favourable conditions for the rapid building of socialism. Having adopted this policy, the Party is now working to get individual peasants gradually to join the mutual-aid teams, which contain the rudiments of socialist relations, agricultural co-operatives of the lower semi-socialist type and, eventually, co-operatives of the higher socialist type.

149

Being densely populated, the North Vietnamese country-side has only a limited amount of land; implements are antiquated, and labour productivity, consequently, is extremely low. But the simple forms of peasant co-operation, improved methods of cultivation and better management have already produced a higher productivity than the individual farmer can show. Our peasants are aware of this. They have their own revolutionary traditions, boundless confidence in the Party, and respond readily to its calls. The peasants are enthusiastically joining the mutual aid teams and the agricultural co-operatives; they are taking the socialist way. The co-operatives now unite more than 40 per cent of the peasant households.

The consolidation of socialist production relations will, undoubtedly, ensure the advance of agriculture and this, in turn, will further the industrial development without which the countryside cannot get the electric power, the water for irrigation, and the agricultural machinery it needs.

Another task of paramount importance is the *peaceful remoulding of the national bourgeoisie along socialist lines.* In the sphere of economic relations we are pursuing a *policy of compensation,* not of confiscating means of production owned by the national bourgeoisie. In the political sphere the national bourgeoisie have definite rights and their place in the Patriotic Front.*

In the past the colonial status always precluded the national bourgeoisie from becoming an important class force. The imperialists and the feudal lords retarded their development and relegated them to the background. And precisely for this reason a considerable section of them joined the anti-imperialist and anti-feudal struggle and took part in the patriotic war. By virtue of their class nature the national bourgeoisie are reluctant to stop exploiting others and nurture the hope that further development will take place along capitalist lines. But our advance to socialism

* Established in 1955 on the basis of the National United Front of Vietnam. — Ed.

rules out this possibility. The national bourgeoisie realise that they can retain their place in the national family only by agreeing to socialist reforms. Most of them appreciate that their future is bound up with participation in the socialist reconstruction of society.

The results in the sphere of education are most gratifying. Over 85 per cent of the population was illiterate under French rule, whereas now illiteracy has in the main been wiped out in North Vietnam.

Below is a table showing the number of pupils and students in educational establishments:

	1939 Whole of Indo-China	1959—60 North Vietnam alone
Universities	582 students	7,518 students
Technical schools	438 pupils	18,100 pupils
General education schools	540,000 pupils	1,522,000 pupils

The following data relates to the health service:

	1939 North and Central Vietnam	1959 North Vietnam alone
Hospitals	54	138
Village health centres	138	1,500
Doctors	86	292
Nurses	968	6,020
Sanitary and public health personnel in the countryside.		169,000

Our achievements to date are clear proof that it is the aim of socialism to abolish worry and poverty from the lives of the working people, to provide them with employment, to make them happy and prosperous. It is the duty of the Party and the people to exert every effort to produce more, faster, better and with more economy.

On the basis of the progress made, we shall now have to draw up long-term plans.

How is our success to be explained?

The explanation is to be sought in the fact that our Party, which has always *taken a firm class proletarian stand and placed the interests of the people above everything else,* has applied Marxist-Leninist theory correctly to Vietnamese conditions and charted a correct political course. The Party has ceaselessly combated the reformist tendencies of the bourgeoisie and the political adventurism of the petty-bourgeois sections in the national movement, the left phraseology used by the Trotskyites in the working-class movement, and the right and "left" deviations in the Party, both in hammering out and in implementing the strategic and tactical lines at the different stages. Marxism-Leninism helped us to withstand all the revolutionary movement, but to keep a firm hold on the storms and stresses. This enabled our Party to take were the leadership and repulse the onslaughts of the bourgeoisie, who were contending with us for the leading role.

Guided by Marxist-Leninist theory, we realised that in a backward agrarian country such as Vietnam, the overriding national issue was the peasant question, that the national revolution was, basically, a peasant revolution, carried out under the leadership of the working class, and that people's power was worker-peasant power. Basing itself on this teaching, our Party *correctly understood and solved the peasant question and worked indefatigably to strengthen the worker-peasant alliance* at each stage. It combated the right and "left" deviations which underestimated the role of the peasants in the revolution, denying that they were the chief ally of the proletariat, and that as the strongest numerical force they, together with the proletariat, would build social-ism. Both the right and the "left" failed to perceive that the worker-peasant alliance was the backbone of the National Front and people's power. The Party's revolutionary experience illustrates that its correct decisions, reflecting the aspirations of the peasants and strengthening the alliance of the working class and peasantry, have always accelerated development of the revolution.

The Party succeeded in *rallying* all the patriotic and progressive forces into the *United Front of Vietnam* and in establishing unity of the people in the anti-imperialist and anti-feudal struggle. And with the workers and peasants as the main force in the national bloc, their alliance has formed the basis of the National Front. In matters concerning the formation, consolidation and development of the National Front, the Party always combated sectarianism, solationism and unprincipled compromises. Thirty years of experience in uniting the national forces show that only by combating these tendencies can we ensure for the Marxist-Leninist Party the leading role in the National Front and reinforce its worker-peasant base.

Our Party grew and developed in the favourable international conditions created by the victory of the Great October Revolution. The achievements of the Party and the people are inseparable from the fraternal support accorded us by the Soviet Union, People's China and the other socialist countries, the international Communist and workers' movement and the national-liberation movement and also the peace movement. We were able to surmount all difficulties and lead the people to glorious victories because the Party *did not divorce the revolutionary movement in its own country from the revolutionary movement of the world proletariat and the national-liberation movement of the oppressed people.*

We are sincerely grateful to the Communist Parties of the Soviet Union and China, who have helped us to become a party of the new type. We shall always remember the generous support given to our Party and the people in their revolutionary struggle by the Communist Parties of the Soviet Union, China and France.

Successfully building socialism in North Vietnam and fighting for the reunification of the country, the Vietnam Workers' Party will continue its efforts to strengthen the international solidarity of the working class. It will do all in its power to consolidate the might of the socialist camp headed by the Soviet Union, to educate the people in the spirit of socialist internationalism, which is inseparable from genuine patriotism, to extend contacts between the revolutionary movement in its own country and the struggle waged by the working masses and the oppressed people in other lands for world peace, democracy, independence and socialism.

Much will have to be done to fulfil this difficult but honourable task. The Party must raise the level of its ideological and organisational work, ensure the growth of the Party organisations, and train new members from all sections of the working people, first and foremost the working class, with the object of strengthening its proletarian core.

Party functionaries should make a deeper study of Marxist-Leninist theory, deepen their class proletarian consciousness, study the laws of development of the Vietnamese revolution, comply with revolutionary ethics, vigorously combat individualism, strengthen proletarian collectivism, be industrious, thrifty, work in close contact with the masses, and place the interests of the revolution and the people above everything.

Socialist construction in North Vietnam demands from our members that they work tirelessly to raise their cultural, scientific and technological level.

The Party is confronted with the task of giving better guidance in all spheres of activity. The Labour Youth Union should be the Party's right hand in organising and educating the rising generation in the spirit of fidelity to the cause of building socialism and communism. The trade unions should be a school of administration, economic management and cultural guidance for the working class. Under the leadership of the Party the agricultural co-operatives should become shock brigades in the battle waged by the millions of peasants to produce more and more, a prosperous, socialist countryside. It is the duty of our People's Army to work assiduously to raise its political level, assimilate techniques and strengthen its military preparedness, and be ever ready to uphold the independence of the country, to defend the peaceful, constructive labour of the people.

Under the banner of Marxism-Leninism our invincible Party, confident of the victory of the army of Communists, will close its ranks. It is leading the working people boldly towards new victories in socialist construction and for the reunification of the country.

The Path Which Led Me to Leninism

*(Published in the Soviet review "P r o b l e m s
o f t h e E a s t, April, 1960.)*

After World War 1, I made my living in Paris, now as a retoucher at a photographer's, now as painter of "Chinese antiquities" (made in France !). I used to distribute leaflets denouncing the crimes committed by the French colonialists in Vietnam.

At that time, I supported the October Revolution only instinctively, not yet grasping all its historic importance. I loved and admired Lenin because he was a great patriot who liberated his compatriots; until then, I had read none of his books.

The reason for my joining the French Socialist Party was that these "ladies and gentlemen" — as I called my comrades at that moment — had shown their sympathy towards me, towards the struggle of the oppressed peoples. But I understood neither what was a party, a trade union, nor what was socialism nor communism.

Heated discussion were then taking place in the branches of the Socialist Party about the question whether the Socialist Party should remain in the Second International, should a Two and a half International be founded or should the Socialist Party join Lenin's Third International? I attended the meetings regularly, twice or thrice a week, and attentively listened to the discussion. First, I could not understand thoroughly. Why were the discussions so heated? Either with the Second, Two and a half or Third International, the revolution could be waged. What was the use of arguing? As for the first International, what had become of it?

What I wanted most to know — and this precisely was not debated in the meetings — was: which International sides with the peoples of colonial countries?

I raised this question — the most important in my opinion — in a meeting. Some comrades answered: It is the Third, not the Second International. And a comrade gave me Lenin's "Thesis on the national and colonial questions" published by *l'Humanité* to read.

There were political terms difficult to understand in this thesis. But by dint of reading it again and again, finally I could grasp the main part of it. What emotion, enthusiasm, clearsightedness and confidence it instilled into me! I wept for joy. Though sitting alone in my room, I shouted out aloud as if addressing large crowds: "Dear martyrs, compatriots! This is what we need, this is the path to our liberation!"

After that I had entire confidence in Lenin, in the Third International.

Formerly, during the meetings of the Party branch, I only listened to the discussion; I had a vague belief that all the speakers were logical, and could not differentiate as to who were right and who were wrong. But from then on, I also plunged into the debates and discussed with fervour. Though I still lacked French words to express all my thoughts, I smashed the allegations attacking Lenin and the Third International with no less vigour. My only argument was: "If you do not condemn colonialism, if you do not side with the colonial people, what kind of revolution are you waging?"

Not only did I take part in the meetings of my own Party branch, but I also went to other Party branches to lay down "my position". Comrades Marcel Cachin, Vaillant Couturier, Monmousseau and many others helped me to broaden my knowledge. Finally, at the Tours Congress, I voted with them for our joining the Third International.

At first, patriotism, not yet communism, led me to have confidence in Lenin, in the Third International. Step by step, along the struggle, by studying Marxism-Leninism parallel with participation in practical activities, I gradually came upon the fact that only socialism and communism can liberate the oppressed nations and the working people throughout the world from slavery.

There is a legend, in our country as well as in China, of the miraculous "Book of the Wise". When facing great difficulties, one opens it and finds a way out. Leninism is not only a miraculous "Book of the Wise", a compass for us Vietnamese revolutionaries and people: it is also the radiant sun illuminating our path to final victory, to socialism and communism.

ANSWERS TO THE BRITISH DAILY WORKER

(The D a i l y   W o r k e r, London, July 1, 1965)

Question: What is the main cause of the South Vietnamese people's struggle?

Answer: The main cause of the South Vietnamese people's patriotic struggle is the barbarous aggression of the United States imperialists, by which they are trying to turn the southern part of our country into a new-type colony and a military base for the expansion of their war of aggression in realising their aim of world domination.

Question: What are the basic aims of the National Liberation Front in South Vietnam? What is the relation between the policy of the Democratic Republic of Vietnam and that of the South Vietnam Liberation Front?

Answer: The programme of the South Vietnam National Front for Liberation has clearly specified its principal aims. These are to struggle against aggressive United States imperialism, to liberate South Vietnam, to achieve independence, democracy, peace and neutrality and advance step by step towards the reunification of the country. The National Front for Liberation is an organisation of the patriotic movement, set up by the masses of the people. It is the leader, the organiser of the South Vietnamese people's struggle against United States imperialism to recover national independence. It is the only genuine representative of the South Vietnamese people. It is the sacred duty of the whole people of Vietnam to support the South Vietnamese people's liberation struggle, waged under the leadership of the Front. We respect the policies of the Front and hold that the two zones must take their respective characteristics into account, understand each other, restore normal relations between them and gradually achieve national reunification.

Vietnam is one. The Vietnamese are one people. Our entire people have the duty of opposing foreign aggression and defending the fatherland.

Question: Do you still think that the Geneva Agreements provide the basis for the solution of the war in Vietnam?

Answer: Yes, the Geneva Agreements are still the basis for the peaceful solution of the war.

Question: What in your view are the most important provisions of the Geneva Agreements?

Answer: I think that the most important provisions are: the sovereignty, independence, unity and territorial integrity of Vietnam must be respected; no military base under the control of a foreign state may be established in Vietnam; Vietnam shall not join any military alliance; democratic freedoms must be guaranteed to create favourable conditions for the restoration of normal relations between the North and the South of Vietnam with a view to the reunification of the country.

Question: What do you consider to be necessary at the present time for the implementation of the Geneva Agreements?

Answer: The 1954 Geneva Agreements on Vietnam are an important international document. All countries participating in the Geneva Conference, including the United States, must respect these agreements and implement them correctly. A country which is a Co-Chairman of the Geneva conference, like Britain, should all the more respect its obligations and carry them out correctly.

Question: What have you to say about the latest proposal of Mr. Harold Wilson for a Commonwealth mission?

Answer: Mr. Wilson has not correctly carried out his obligations as a Co-Chairman of the 1954 Geneva Conference on Vietnam. He has tried to support United States imperialist aggression in Vietnam. He cannot engage in peace negotiations since he has himself supported the United

States policy of aggression and expansion of the war.

Question: What special message would you like to give the British progressive movement and the British people?

Answer: On behalf of the Vietnamese people, I convey our cordial greetings to the British working class, intellectuals, progressive politicans and the British people in general who have warmly supported our just struggle against the United States imperialist aggressors and demanded that the British Government should correctly carry out its obligations as Co-Chairman of the Geneva Conference. I also send warm greetings to the readers of the *Daily Worker.*

REPLY TO PROFESSOR LINUS PAULING

(Hanoi, November 17, 1965)

Dear Professor Linus Pauling,

I sincerely thank you for having kindly sent me the text of the Appeal issued by eight Nobel Peace Prize recipients on the Vietnam question.

The Vietnamese people are by nature freedom and peace-loving and their earnest aspiration is to build up a peaceful, united, independent, democratic, prosperous and strong Vietnam.

Our people, in the North as well as in the South, have struggled hard for the thorough implementation of the 1954 Geneva Agreements on Vietnam. But the U.S. imperialists have brazenly trampled underfoot these agreements, plotting to turn South Vietnam into a U.S. new-type colony and military base, with a view to dominating South-East Asia and preparing for a new world war. They have sabotaged the peaceful reunification of Vietnam and have set up an extremely ruthless fascist regime in South Vietnam, where hundreds of thousands of people have been arrested, tortured, jailed and massacred, and millions of others herded into concentration camps of various forms. The U.S. imperialists have used South Vietnam as a springboard for war activities in Laos and for daily provocations against the Kingdom of Cambodia. Since 1961, they have been waging a so-called "special war" in South Vietnam. But not willing to bow to the invaders our Southern compatriots have been struggling heroically against the U.S. aggressors and their henchmen and are scoring ever greater victories.

Having suffered heavy defeats in their "special war" the U.S. imperialists have, in addition to the existing 600,000 puppet troops, brought into South Vietnam 200,000 U.S. and satellite troops, in order to expand their war of aggression. This constitutes a greave threat to the security of the peoples of South-East Asia and to world peace.

They are using South Vietnam as a testing ground for a new type war of aggression as well as for new kinds of modern weapons and means of warfare, which will be eventually employed in other countries with a view to suppressing the national liberation movement and establishing U.S. rule over the world.

At present, most barbarous means of warfare such as napalm bombs, phosphorous bombs, toxic chemicals, poison gas, etc., are being used by the U.S. aggressors to massacre our compatriots in South Vietnam. Their Seventh Fleet and B. 52 planes are bombing, shelling and razing to the ground South Vietnamese villages and hamlets.

At the same time, in utter defiance of public opinion in the U.S.A. and in the world, they have unremittingly pursued their policy of "escalation" against North Vietnam by frenziedly launching daily air raids on bridges, roads, dams, state farms, enterprises, schools, hospitals, churches, etc.

The Vietnamese people must resolutely struggle against the U.S. imperialist aggressore in order to defend themselves, to uphold their most sacred national rights and at the same time to contribute to the preservation of peace in Asia and in the world.

For several months, while frantically intensifying and expanding its aggressive war in Vietnam, the U.S. Government has been clamouring that it does not intend to expand the war and is ready to negotiate.

The peoples of the world, including the American people, have come to realise more and more clearly that this is but deceitful talk on the part of the U.S. rulers, whose policy is to negotiate from a position of strength, to perpetrate ever more horrible massacres and cause ever greater devastation, in order to compel the Vietnamese people to lay down their arms and give up their legitimate aspirations.

The Vietnamese people from the North to the South, find this U.S. imperialist policy of aggression and enslavement wholly unacceptable. Genuine peace is absolutely inseparable from genuine national freedom and independence.

It is obvious that the U.S. imperialists are the aggressors and the Vietnamese people the victims of aggression.

U.S. aggression is the sole root and direct cause of the serious situation prevailing at present in Vietnam and in South East Asia. Consequently, it is our view that the most correct way to a peaceful settlement of the Vietnam problem is the one expounded in the March 22, 1965 statement of the South Vietnam National Front for Liberation, the only authentic representative of the South Vietnamese people, and in the four-point stand of the Government of the Democratic Republic of Vietnam.

These four points are:

1. Recognition of the basic national rights of the Vietnamese people: peace, independence, sovereignty, unity and territorial integrity. In accordance with the Geneva Agreements, the U.S. Government must withdraw from South Vietnam all U.S. troops, military personnel and weapons of all kinds, dismantle all U.S. military bases there, cancel its "military alliance" with the South Vietnam authorities. The U.S. Government must end its policy of intervention and aggression in South Vietnam. In accordance with the Geneva Agreements the U.S. Government must stop its acts of war against North Vietnam, cease all encroachments on the territory and sovereignty of the Democratic Republic of Vietnam.

2. Pending peaceful reunification, while Vietnam is still temporarily divided into two zones, the military provisions of the 1954 Geneva Agreements on Vietnam must be strictly respected; the two zones must refrain from joining any military alliance with foreign military bases, troops and military personnel on their respective territory.

3. The internal affairs of South Vietnam must be settled by the people of South Vietnam themselves, in accordance

with the programme of the South Vietnam National Front for Liberation, without any foreign interference.

4. The peaceful reunification of Vietnam is to be settled by the Vietnamese people in both zones, without any foreign interference.

I hope that, in the interest of peace and justice, you, dear Professor Linus Pauling and the other signatories to the appeal, will continue to exert your influence and, together with the American and world peoples, strive to expose the U.S. imperialists' schemes of war provocation and aggression and compel them to put an end to their criminal war against our people so that peace in Vietnam may be restored.

The war of aggression being carried out by the U.S. Government in Vietnam causes not only great sufferings and sacrifices to our people but also heavy losses to the American people in human lives, and material resources. This war also besmears the honour of the United States.

It is precisely for that reason that, recently, many progressive sections of the American people, including hundreds of thousands of American youth and students, thousands of professors, scientists, writers, artists, and many religious authorities have courageously come out against the Johnson Administration's war of aggression, staging protest demonstrations and rallies, or expressing their resolute refusal to join the army and take part in the massacre of the Vietnamese people. Our people highly value this struggle of the American people, and are deeply moved by the valiant sacrifices of Mrs. Helga Herz and of the other peace fighters — Norman Morrison, Roger Laporte and Celene Jankowski.

I take this opportunity to express my heartfelt thanks to the American people who are resolutely struggling against the U.S. imperialists' war of aggression in Vietnam. I also wish to convey to the martyrs' families the love and admiration of the Vietnamese people.

Please accept my high regards to you, dear Professor, and to your fellow recipients of the Nobel Peace Prize.

HO CHI MINH

LETTER TO HEADS OF STATE OF THE SOVIET UNION, THE
PEOPLE'S REPUBLIC OF CHINA AND THE OTHER SOCIALIST
COUNTRIES

(Hanoi, January 24, 1966)

Dear Comrade President,

I have the honour to call your attention to the war of
aggression waged by the U.S. imperialists in our country
Vietnam.

As is known to you, over the past eleven years and more
the U.S. imperialists have been seriously sabotaging the
1954 Geneva Agreements and preventing the peaceful reunification of Vietnam in an attempt to turn South Vietnam
into a U.S. new-type colony and military base. They are
now waging a war of aggression and barbarously repressing
the patriotic struggle of our fellow countrymen in the South.
At the same time, they try to draw experiences from this
war to repress the national liberation movement in other
countries.

In an endeavour to get out of the quagmire in South
Vietnam, the U.S. imperialists have massively increased
the strength of the U.S. expeditionary force and sent in
troops from a number of their satellites to wage direct
aggression in South Vietnam. They have also launched air
attacks on the Democratic Republic of Vietnam, an independent and soveriegn country and a member of the socialist
camp.

While intensifying and extending the war of aggression
in Vietnam the U.S. imperialists are clamouring about their
"desire for peace" and their "readiness to engage in unconditional discussions" in the hope of fooling world and American public opinion. Recently the Johnson administration

has initiated the so-called "search for peace" and put forward a fourteen-point proposal. As an excuse for its war of aggression in South Vietnam it claims that it is "keeping its commitments" to the Saigon puppet administration, it slanders the patriotic struggle of the people of South Vietnam, calling it "an aggression by North Vietnam". This deceitful contention can in no way rub out the solemn declaration made by the United States in Geneva in 1954 that it will" refrain from the threat or the use of force to disturb them" (i.e. the Geneva Agreements). Still less can President Johnson's hypocritical allegations conceal the U.S. crimes in Vietnam.

The United States talks about respecting the Geneva Agreements. But one of the main provisions of the said agreements bans the introduction of foreign troops into Vietnam. If the United States really respects the agreements, it must withdraw all U.S. and satellite troops from Vietnam.

It is crystal clear that the United States is the aggressor who is trampling underfoot the Vietnamese soil. The people of South Vietnam are the victims of aggression and are fighting in self-defence. If the United States really wants peace, it must recognise the South Vietnam National Front for Liberation as the sole genuine representative of the people of South Vietnam and engage in negotiations with it. In accordance with the aspirations of the people of South Vietnam and the spirit of the 1954 Geneva Agreements on Vietnam the National Front for Liberation is fighting to achieve independence, democracy, peace and neutrality in South Vietnam, and to advance towards the peaceful reunification of the fatherland. If the United States really respects the right to self-determination of the people of South Vietnam, it cannot but approve this correct programme of the National Front for Liberation.

The fourteen points of the United States boil down in essence to this: the United States is trying hard to cling to South Vietnam, to maintain there the puppet administration rigged up by it and to perpetuate the partition of Vietnam.

In his January 12, 1966 message read before the U.S. Congress, President Johnson affirmed that it was the policy of the United States not to pull out of South Vietnam, and he forced the Vietnamese people to choose between "peace" and the "ravages of a conflict". That is an impudent threat, an attempt to impose on the Vietnamese people the conditions of the so-called U.S. "unconditional discussions".

The Vietnamese people will never submit to the U.S. imperialists' threats.

At the very moment when the U.S. Government puts forward the so-called new "peace efforts", it is frantically increasing the U.S. strength in South Vietnam. It is stepping up terrorist raids, resorting to the "scorched earth" policy — burning all, destroying all, killing all — using napalm bombs, poison gases and toxic chemicals to burn down villages and massacre the civilian population in vast areas of South Vietnam.

I strongly protest against such extremely barbarous methods of warfare. I earnestly call on all peace-loving governments and peoples the world over to resolutely stay the hands of the U.S. war criminals.

The United States keeps sending its planes on espionage flights in preparation for new air attacks on the Democratic Republic of Vietnam.

On the other hand it is launching air attacks on many areas in the Kingdom of Laos, and multiplying armed provocations against the Kingdom of Cambodia, thus posing an even more serious menace to peace in Indochina.

Obviously, the U.S. "search for peace" is only designed to conceal its schemes for an intensified war of aggression. The Johnson administration stand remains: aggression and expansion of the war.

To settle the Vietnamese question, the Government of the Democratic Republic of Vietnam has put forward the four-point stand which is an expression of the essential provisions of the 1954 Geneva Agreements on Vietnam. This is a stand of peace.

Having gone through over twenty years of war, the Vietnamese people desire peace more eagerly than any one else to build their life. But real peace can by no means be dissociated from genuine independence. So long as the U.S. aggressor force still remains on our soil, our people will resolutely fight against it. If the U.S. Government really wants a peaceful settlement, it must accept the four-point stand of the Government of the Democratic Republic of Vietnam, and prove this by actual deeds, it must end unconditionally and for good all bombing raids and other war acts against the Democratic Republic of Vietnam. Only in this way can a political solution to the Vietnamese problem be envisaged.

Dear Comrade President,

So far, in the spirit of international solidarity, the people and Government of your country have been giving wholehearted support and assistance to the Vietnamese people in their struggle against the U.S. imperialist aggressors for the defence of their independence and freedom. On behalf of the Vietnamese people and Government of the Democratic Republic of Vietnam, I wish to express our deep gratitude to the people and Government of your country.

In face of the extremely serious situation brought about by the United States in Vietnam, I firmly believe that the people and Government of your country will extend increased support and assistance to our people's just struggle, resolutely condemn the U.S. Government's sham peace tricks, and check in time all new perfidious manoeuvres of the United States in Vietnam and Indochina.

I take this opportunity to renew to you, comrade President, the assurances of my highest consideration.

Ho Chi Minh
President
of the Democratic Republic of Vietnam

Reply to President Lyndon B. Johnson

To His Excellency Mr. Lyndon B. Johnson
President,
United States of America
Your Excellency,

On February 10, 1967, I received your message. This is my reply.

Vietnam is thousands of miles away from the United States. The Vietnamese people have never done any harm to the United States. But contrary to the pledges made by its representative at the 1954 Geneva Conference, the U.S. Government has ceaselessly intervened in Vietnam, it has unleashed and intensified the war of aggression in South Vietnam with a view to prolonging the partition of Vietnam and turning South Vietnam into a neo-colony and military base of the United States. For over two years now, the U.S. Government has, with its air and naval forces, carried the war to the Democratic Republic of Vietnam, an independent and sovereign country.

The U.S. Government has committed war crimes, crimes against peace and against mankind. In South Vietnam, half a million U.S. and satellite troops have resorted to the most inhuman weapons and the most barbarous methods of warfare, such as napalm, toxic chemicals and gases, to massacre our compatriots, destroy crops, and raze villages to the ground. In North Vietnam, thousands of U.S. aircraft have dropped hundreds of thousands of tons of bombs, destroying towns, villages, factories, roads, bridges, dykes, dams, and even churches, pagodas, hospitals, schools. In your message you apparently deplored the sufferings and destructions in Vietnam. May I ask you: Who has perpetrated these monstrous crimes? It is the U.S. and satellite troops.

The U.S. Government is entirely responsible for the extremely serious situation in Vietnam.

The U.S. war of aggression against the Vietnamese people constitutes a challenge to the countries of the socialist camp, a threat to the national independence movement and a serious danger to peace in Asia and the world.

The Vietnamese people deeply love independence, freedom and peace. But in the face of the U.S. aggression, they have risen up, united as one man, fearless of scarifices and hardships: they are determined to carry on their Resistance until they have won genuine independence and freedom and true peace. Our just cause enjoys strong sympathy and support from the peoples of the whole world including broad sections of the American people.

The U.S. Government has unleashed the war of aggression in Vietnam. It must cease this aggression. That is the only way to the restoration of peace. The U.S. Government must stop definitively and unconditionally its bombing raids and all other acts of war against the Democratic Republic of Vietnam: withdraw from South Vietnam all U.S. and satellite troops; recognise the South Vietnam National Front for Liberation: and let the Vietnamese people settle themselves their own affairs. Such is the basic content of the four-point stand of the Government of the Democratic Republic of Vietnam, which embodies the essential principles and provisions of the 1954 Geneva Agreements on Vietnam. It is the basis of a correct political solution to the Vietnam problem.

In your message, you suggested direct talks between the Democratic Republic of Vietnam and the United States. If the U.S. Government really wants these talks, it must first of all stop unconditionally its bombing raids and all other acts of war against the Democratic Republic of Vietnam. It is only after the unconditional cessation of the U.S. bombing raids and all other acts of war against the Democratic Republic of Vietnam that the Democratic Republic of Vietnam and the United States could enter into talks and discuss questions concerning the two sides.

171

The Vietnamese people will never submit to force: they will never accept talks under the threat of bombs.

Our cause is absolutely just. It is to be hoped that the U.S. Government will act in accordance with reason.

TESTAMENT

May 10, 1969

Our people's struggle against U.S. aggression, for national salvation, may have to go through even more difficulties and sacrifices, but we are bound to win total victory.

This is a certainty.

I intend, when that comes, to tour both North and South to congratulate our heroic compatriots, cadres and combatants, and visit old people and our beloved youth and children.

Then, on behalf of our people, I will go to the fraternal countries of the socialist camp and friendly countries in the world, and thank them for their wholehearted support and assistance to our people's patriotic struggle against U.S. aggression.

Tu Fu, the well-known Chinese poet of the T'ang period, wrote: "Few have ever reached the age of seventy."

This year, being seventy-nine, I count among those "few"; still, my mind has remained very lucid, though my health has somewhat declined in comparison with previous years. When one is on the wrong side of seventy, health deteriorates with age. This is no wonder.

But who can say how much longer I shall be able to serve the revolution, the Fatherland and the people?

I therefore leave these few lines in anticipation of the day when I shall go and join Karl Marx, V.I. Lenin and other elder revolutionaries; this way, our people throughout the country, our comrades in the Party, and our friends in the world will not be taken by surprise.

First about the Party: Thanks to its close unity and total dedication to the working class, the people and the Fatherland, our Party has been able, since its founding, to unite, organize and lead our people from success to success in a resolute struggle.

Unity is an extremely precious tradition of our Party and people. All comrades, from the Central Committee down to the cell, must preserve the unity and oneness of mind in the Party as the apple of their eye.

Within the Party, to achieve broad democracy and to practise self-criticism and criticism regularly and seriously is the best way to consolidate and further solidarity and unity. Comradely affection should prevail.

Ours is a Party in power. Each Party member, each cadre, must be deeply imbued with revolutionary morality, and show industry, thrift, integrity, uprightness, total dedication to public interests and complete selflessness. Our Party should preserve absolute purity and prove worthy of its role as leader and very loyal servant of the people.

About the working youth union members and our young people: On the whole they are excellent; they are always ready to come forward, fearless of difficulties and eager for progress. The Party must foster their revolutionary virtues and train them as our successors, both "red" and "expert," in the building of socialism.

Training and educating future revolutionary generations is of great importance and necessity.

About our labouring people: In the plains as in the mountain areas, they have for ages endured hardships, feudal and colonial oppression and exploitation; they have moreover experienced many years of war.

Yet, our people have shown great heroism, courage, enthusiasm and industriousness. They have always followed the Party since it came into being, with unqualified loyalty.

The Party must work out a very effective plan for economic and cultural development constantly to raise the living standard of the people.

About the resistance war against U.S. aggression: It may

drag on. Our compatriots may have to face new sacrifices in property and life. Whatever may happen, we must keep firm our resolve to fight the U.S. aggressors till total victory.

Our rivers, our mountains, our people will always be;
The American aggressors defeated, we will build a country
ten times more beautiful.

Whatever difficulties and hardships may be ahead, our people are sure of total triumph. The U.S. imperialists shall have to quit. Our Fatherland shall be reunified. Our compatriots in the North and in the South shall be reunited under the same roof. We, a small nation, will have earned the unique honour of defeating, through a heroic struggle, two big imperialisms — the French and the American — and making a worthy contribution to the national liberation movement.

About the world communist movement: Having devoted my whole life to the revolution, I am proud of the growth of the international communist and workers' movement as well as grieved at the dissensions now dividing the fraternal parties. I hope that our Party will do its best to contribute effectively to the restoration of unity among the fraternal parties on the basis of Marxism-Leninism and proletarian internationalism, in a way which conforms to both reason and sentiment. I am sure that the fraternal parties and countries will have to unite again.

About personal matters: All my life, I have served the Fatherland, the revolution and the people with all my heart and strength. If I should now depart from this world, I would regret nothing, except not being able to serve longer and more.

When I am gone, grand funerals should be avoided so as not to waste the people's time and money.

Finally, to the whole people, the whole Party, the whole

175

army, to my nephews and nieces, the youth and children, leave my boundless love.

I also convey my cordial greetings to our comrades and friends, to the youth and children in the world.

My ultimate wish is that our whole Party and people closely joining their efforts, build a peaceful, unified, independent, democratic and prosperous Viet Nam, and make a worthy contribution to the world revolution.

HO CHI MINH